ONE WORD
PRAYERS
for mums

ONE WORD PRAYERS

for mums

Lirika Davis

Scripture quotations are taken from the *Holy Bible*, New Living Translation, copyright © 1996, 2004, 2015 by Tyndale House Foundation. Used by permission of Tyndale House Publishers, Inc., Carol Stream, Illinois 60188. All rights reserved.

Other versions are marked: Amplified: Scripture quotations taken from the Amplified® Bible (AMP). Copyright © 2015 by The Lockman Foundation. Used by permission. www.Lockman.org; ESV: The Holy Bible, English Standard Version® (ESV®). Copyright © 2001 by Crossway, a publishing ministry of Good News Publishers. All rights reserved; KJV: Scripture quotations from The Authorized (King James) Version. Rights in the Authorized Version in the United Kingdom are vested in the Crown. Reproduced by permission of the Crown's patentee, Cambridge University Press; NET: Scripture quoted by permission. Quotations designated (NET) are from the NET Bible® copyright ©1996-2016 by Biblical Studies Press, L.L.C. netbible.com All rights reserved; NIV: New International Version® Anglicised, NIV® Copyright © 1979, 1984, 2011 by Biblica, Inc.® Used by permission. All rights reserved worldwide; NKJV: Scripture taken from the New King James Version®. Copyright © 1982 by Thomas Nelson. Used by permission. All rights reserved. *The Message*: copyright © 1993, 1994, 1995, 1996, 2000, 2001, 2002 by Eugene H. Peterson. Used by permission of NavPress. All rights reserved. Represented by Tyndale House Publishers, Inc.; TPT: Scripture quotations marked TPT are from The Passion Translation®. Copyright © 2017, 2018 by Passion & Fire Ministries, Inc. Used by permission. All rights reserved. ThePassionTranslation.com.

Cover design by Sara Venner
Internals designed by Xenia Knight
Edited by Katie Carter at yourwordsrefined.com
Printed in the UK
ISBN: 978-1-9160069-0-4

FOR ALL TIRED AND NEVER
GIVING UP MUMS

Contents

Introduction

As long as there is life on earth, as long as we are here, there will be a need for us to pray – to talk with our creator. I want to be better at prayer and I have a feeling I am not alone in this.

Throughout my journey as a Christian woman, I have struggled with prayer. I don't know why but I don't seem to find the right time for it and when I do I somehow lose concentration, or feel nothing and get discouraged. I question myself if I have enough faith, if I repent with enough sorrow, if I say the right words, if I pray with enough reverence. When prayers don't seem to work, I wonder if praying is a waste of time. You can see I complicate prayer, and as a result I avoid it.

But I do believe that the main reason we don't pray is because prayer is powerful and effective, and the enemy of our souls knows that far better than we do, so he does whatever he can to keep us passive and slothful about it. A believer without prayer is a coasting believer – wandering around and getting tossed and turned by every wind of the world. Without prayer, a believer is powerless and limited.

We may be stuck at 'saying our prayers each night' or only praying in an 'emergency'. These prayers are not wrong but if we want to see miracles, wonders and the impossible we can't afford to be casual about our prayer life. We can't be timid. We must pray fervently and boldly. To combat the devil and his strategies we need to pray without ceasing and with purpose. We need to align ourselves with our Lord.

We can start simply. We can start our prayer journey with one-word prayers. Prayers for joy, peace, salvation... I am sure we can all think of one word that we'd like our children to become, one word that we'd like our actions to illustrate or one word we want our lives to head towards. Perhaps we struggle with fear, lies or comparison... again, just start with one word.

This is how I'm developing my prayer life and why I've written this devotional. I want to help and encourage us to pray without getting tangled in our methods and lists. And so I invite you to focus on one word each day and ask the Holy Spirit to guide and help you start speaking with God (for he knows what your kids, your health, your home and your community needs).

These prayers are also specifically for our children. When writing each devotion, I kept my heart, eyes and ears open to the things my children were struggling with, and things that I desired for them to develop based on God's Word. That was my starting point and it can be yours too.

In an effort to make this a strong habit, I continued to meditate on the word I was praying and found Bible verses connected with it, which helped me to pray prayers based on the promises of God in his Word. I became curious about the meaning of the words in ancient Hebrew and Greek and dug a little bit deeper. The Hebrew and the Greek languages are so rich and expressive, so when you see me expanding the meaning of the words, remember that there are many other words that can be used to describe the same word. I have used the ones that have been the closest to my understanding of the word I was praying (I used Vine's Expository Dictionary of the Old and New Testament Words (Super Value Series, Hardcover, 2003) and www.biblestudytools.com/dictionaries/).

I soon found that all these things added up and created meaningful prayers for me to pray, based on my children's needs and the assurance and promises of the Word of God. Let the prayers in this book be just the start. Expand on them as you speak and listen to your heavenly father.

[Why 40 days?]

Prayer is about learning to trust God with what matters most to us. We, by nature, are 'control freaks'. Prayer helps us to let go of control and hold onto God. Biblically, all the people who God prepared for great works (Jesus, Moses, Elijah etc) or took on a journey of change and repentance (People of Ninevah through Jonah), he used this period of 40 days to accomplish some foundational groundwork. Science and psychology confirm this number too – if we want to set a new habit, we should aim to keep it up for 40 days to establish it.

[Before you start]

I just wanted to say a few words before you start, dear one.

Have a specific place where you go to pray. It can be a chair, a quiet room, a corner table, on the floor... anywhere where you can pray without disturbance. Trust me, this alone will help with time and focus.

As I mentioned above, prayer has many oppositions. Pray for God to help you. Pray for strength, alertness, guidance and wisdom. Do ask a friend to join you or mention you are starting a 40-day devotional so that you can be accountable and they can cheer you on. I am praying and standing with you also.

1

Joy

We are living in a time that boasts some of the best technological advancements and the wealthiest countries in the history of the world. Yet, if we look at the latest UNICEF reports on the wellbeing of children, it seems that we are raising a generation of joyless children. Why?

Children are children, no matter their time in history. Their need for love, parental attention and affection does not change with the change of times. They need to belong, to feel secure; to be helped to develop and form an inner strength to cope with life and its different pressures.

It may not be true for you, but I've noticed that the joyful sounds that came from gardens and playgrounds have been largely replaced with silence while earphones transmit noise from the latest games, music and film. The issue with staying and playing inside is that it makes us all feel we have each other's company, but in fact, we are further from each other. We talk too little about the things that matter the most, we listen distractedly, and we avoid speaking heart to heart. It is my conviction that our lifestyle in these modern days is the main reason we and our children experience little joy.

> 'JOY HAS NOTHING TO DO WITH MATERIAL THINGS, OR WITH A MAN'S OUTWARD CIRCUMSTANCE... A MAN LIVING IN THE LAP OF LUXURY CAN BE WRETCHED, AND A MAN IN THE DEPTHS OF POVERTY CAN OVERFLOW WITH JOY.'
> **WILLIAM BARCLAY**

Some of us may have been taught in church (not necessarily from the pulpit) that if you are too happy then you lack holiness, seriousness and humility. But the Bible does not teach that! It encourages us to 'Always be joyful' (1 Thess. 5:16); that 'the joy of the Lord is [our] strength' (Neh. 8:10), and 'in [his] presence there is fullness of joy' (Psa.16:11, ESV). As believers, we can know that joy is not only possible but essential to our living. For without joy, we are without strength, without hope and without witness. I want my children to grow and mature into joy. The joy that radiates not only on their faces but their hearts and actions too.

[*Pray*]

Jesus, 'You thrill me, LORD, with all you have done for me! I sing for joy because of what you have done.' (Psa. 92:4, NLT). Thank you that I can be 'cheerful with joyous celebration in every season of life' for I am '*united with the Anointed One* -- with you (Phil. 4:4, TPT)!

Heavenly father, I come to you today asking that my children will grow to embrace the joy that comes from you, so that they can 'go out in joy [and] be led into a whole and complete life' (Isa. 55:12, *The Message*). I pray that they will be known as joyful children. I ask that they will become joyful adults and that their lives will reflect a strength that is the result of the joy in you.

Dear God, I ask you to forgive me for the times I've not been such a good example of reflecting your joy in my everyday life. Help me and my family to know that joy – complete joy –comes from walking with you and doing your will. Only then can we remain in your love for us, which is the source of pure joy (John 15:10–11, NIV). Amen.

_____

_____

_____

_____

_____

[Ponder today]

'Joy' (*chara* in Greek and *simchah* in Hebrew) means gladness, mirth, delight and rejoicing. Happiness (as we know it) and divine joy are quite different. Happiness, the one we chase these days, tends to be a product of our circumstances. We say we will be happy 'when we have moved to a new home… if we get that job promotion… after the kids are settled'. But joy is produced by the grace and presence of God; it does not require that everything in our lives is in line and well, for it rarely is. The joy that the Bible speaks of comes from knowing that we are loved and esteemed by God (Isa. 43:1). His grace and mercy assure us that we can have joy in our lives no matter our circumstances because he is in control and works all things for our good (Rom. 8:28).

_____

_____

_____

_____

_____

2

Comparison

'You treat her better than me, he gets away with everything, she's your favourite, he's got more stuff than me.' Perhaps you've heard these arguments between siblings. Almost all the fights between them start because they see themselves in the light of the other.

Comparison is contagious. It's like a silent 'killer' that passes through generations and infects all – unless we deal with it. In the history of the Bible, comparison came right after the disobedience of Adam and Eve in the Garden of Eden. Sadly, it ended with the death of Abel, murdered by his brother (see Gen. 4). We also see issues of comparison between Isaac and Ishmael, Esau and Jacob, Joseph and his brothers, Hannah and Peninnah. Then in the New Testament, we see it between the disciples of John and Jesus, between Peter and John. Today, we can see comparison driving our society and us as people. And social media provokes it all the more.

Unfortunately, our children are not to immune to the comparison trap either. Comparison is not a respecter of age, gender or social position, it comes to all of us and has two purposes in mind: to steal our joy and distract us from our true identity and purpose.

'WE WON'T BE DISTRACTED BY COMPARISON IF WE ARE CAPTIVATED WITH PURPOSE.'
BOB GOFF

We need to see ourselves in the light of God, not in the light of others. Only then can we recognise what we have and know who we truly are. Our focus and energy can be directed back on what God is calling *us* to do. Let's ask God to identify and deal with comparison in our lives so that we, and our children, can be secure in our relationships with Him, with each other and with ourselves.

[_Pray_]

Heavenly father, thank you that you have made us all unique and different on purpose. We are your 'masterpiece', created 'so we can do the good things [you] planned for us long ago' (Eph. 2:10).

Lord, I repent from all comparison and jealousy that I consciously or unconsciously do or have. Teach me to be content with myself and my life and understand that all good gifts come from you. I pray that, as a parent, I will be a good example of cheering on and celebrating others rather than putting them down.

I pray that my family and I will be fulfilled and complete in you so that comparison cannot come in and make us feel inferior or be used as a tool to feel superior to others. Please make us aware of comparison in our home so that we can confess it and open the windows of our hearts to let it out so that it will not take root and produce the fruit of jealousy or pride, dissatisfaction or egotism. I pray that we will be a family that combats comparison with love, thankfulness and celebrations. Amen.

_____

_____

_____

_____

_____

[Ponder today]

'Compare' (*sugkrinó* in Greek and *damah* in Hebrew) portrays this picture of two or more who stand side by side to thoroughly examine themselves in comparison to each other and then to critically judge who is superior among the candidates.

> 'PAY CAREFUL ATTENTION TO YOUR OWN WORK, FOR THEN YOU WILL GET THE SATISFACTION OF A JOB WELL DONE, AND YOU WON'T NEED TO COMPARE YOURSELF TO ANYONE ELSE.' **GALATIANS 6:4, NLT**

Comparing our appearance, our talents, our personalities, our circumstances with others is a vain endeavour that produces no spiritual fruit in our lives. It wastes time. It elevates one and puts another down. And it fails to recognise the diversity in others and how that is a gift for us all to dwell in unity and strength.

_____

_____

_____

_____

_____

3

Listen

Distraction is everywhere. Wherever we turn, something is fighting for our attention. Kids, too, face the same problem. Their minds and attentions are constantly being under the subjection of distraction. Try to have a chat with any child today and you will see their eyes start rolling from side to side almost as soon as the conversation starts; their hands fidgeting and their legs in a 'ready to go' position.

The sad thing is that if you asked our children, they will probably tell you similar answers about trying to have a conversation with us parents. We, too, don't listen intently all the time. Sometimes we may be looking at our children's faces, giving them the impression of listening, but in truth we are thinking of other things: unfinished work, plans for the day, conversations with other people etc. We are not all there. Kids are clever to know when they have our full attention and when we are pretending. So, what happens? They learn to share little (for what's the point of talking when no one is listening) and they start to tune their ears to other voices – the ones that give them full attention. That's a dangerous place to land for young, sponge-like minds. For what we listen to forms our inner voice, which leads our lives.

It's one thing to learn to speak. It's another thing to learn to listen, isn't it? And as we learn from listening, what may we be missing out on when we allow things to distract us from God's and each other's voices?

'HEARING IS AN ACT OF THE SENSES, BUT LISTENING IS AN ACT OF THE WILL.'
ADAM S. MCHUGH

[*Pray*]

Heavenly father, please help me to learn to listen to my children and be all in when they speak. Help me to be graceful and patient with them. Forgive me for rushing sometimes and not giving time to the things of most importance, like listening to my children.

Dear Lord, you say that children are a gift from you (Psa. 127:3). We wouldn't neglect a precious gift usually; we take care and keep it in secure place. Lead me to tend my children with care, handle them with wisdom and cover them constantly with love.

Please help my family to develop the healthy habit of listening well. Help us to grow in wisdom and understanding. Surround us with friends whose voices speak your truth into our lives. Above all, may we listen to you, Lord. Captivate us with your Word and presence, help us to know your voice and hear your heart. Amen.

_____

_____

_____

_____

_____

[Ponder today]

The word 'listen' (*akouo* in Greek and *shema* in Hebrew) means to pay attention, to consider or to focus on, but it also means to respond. Interestingly *shema* means both 'listen' and 'obey'. So it's not a passive word; it's a twofold word. The first is the act of intently listening, for poor listening indicates that the person has low regards for what the other has been saying, or that he is absorbed in his own ideas. The second, after considered listening, is to respond with wisdom, kindness or silence.

'LEAD WITH YOUR EARS,
FOLLOW UP WITH YOUR TONGUE'
JAMES 1:19–21, *THE MESSAGE*

Listening includes the action of intentional hearing and then the action of response to what you learn from that hearing.

_____

_____

_____

_____

_____

4

Decisions

Good character is formed through good decision-making. Our children are people, not robots. I don't know about you, but I've noticed that we can often choose the robot path in educating our children, perhaps because it somehow feels the easier option at the time. We sing this kind of song daily: 'Tidy your room, brush your teeth, do your homework, go to bed...' and if it is met with resistance we add 'do as you are told' or 'because I said so', now in a more effective drumming melody. No wonder we are all exhausted by the end of each day!

> 'I AM CONVINCED THAT EVERY EFFORT MUST BE MADE IN CHILDHOOD TO TEACH THE YOUNG TO USE THEIR OWN MINDS. FOR ONE THING IS SURE: IF THEY DON'T MAKE UP THEIR MINDS, SOMEONE WILL DO IT FOR THEM.'
> **ELEANOR ROOSEVELT**

It's believed that children begin developing the ability to make decisions based on reason from the age of three. We can use encouragement and explanation to help our kids think for themselves. Explaining why they should do certain acts, and encouraging them when they do, is undoubtedly an effective way of teaching them how to make good decisions. We're helping them practise thinking, reasoning and weighing different options, rather than taking orders. Decisions help us all to be responsible – and clarify our values and convictions in practice.

[Pray]

Heavenly father, making decisions isn't always easy. Please help me when I am indecisive or confused about a situation. I pray I will 'Trust in the Lᴏʀᴅ with all [my] heart and lean not on [my] own understanding'; thank you that you will 'make [my] paths straight' when I submit to you (Prov. 3:5–6, NIV).

Forgive me if I've chosen the easier way when it comes to helping my children develop the habit of good decision-making. Help me to have the wisdom and patience to put choices in front of them. Help my children to have a sense of understanding for every action they take so that they can think and choose wisely. Through your grace and leading of the Holy Spirit, please guide us all.

Dear Lord, help my family to be unashamed about asking for the opinions and counselling of others when making decisions that are weighty and of importance. Put around us thoughtful and wise friends who value life-giving decisions – and may we be quick to listen.

_____

_____

_____

_____

_____

[Ponder today]

'Decision' (*diakrino* in Greek and *charuwts* in Hebrew) has different shades of meaning. It expresses the formation of a judgment on a matter under the consideration of all facts. It means the quality of being decided, firm and wise. It speaks of someone who understands a certain issue that is put in front of them and their ability to decide the best way.

Picture a fisherman pulling a big net of fish out of the sea and then sitting down to differentiate and keep the best fish for him and his family. Being decisive is actively considering and weighing between opinions and then deciding for the best outcome.

> 'WISE CHOICES WILL WATCH OVER YOU. UNDERSTANDING WILL KEEP YOU SAFE.' **PROVERBS 2:11**

_____

_____

_____

_____

_____

5

Criticism

'All my love towards my daughter is expressed in criticism,' a friend of mine confessed. She was bold enough to utter what many of us know deep down inside our hearts but hesitate to acknowledge. We all love our children, there is no doubt about that, but how we express that love and care is another matter.

I have heard it said that for every criticism a child receives, they need at least seven compliments to write it off. The sad part of criticism is that it often dresses up as advice and help. 'It is for your good,' we explain ourselves.

> 'LET US BE DIFFERENT
> IN OUR HOMES. LET US
> REALIZE THAT, ALONG
> WITH FOOD, SHELTER,
> AND CLOTHING, WE HAVE
> ANOTHER OBLIGATION
> TO OUR CHILDREN,
> AND THAT IS TO AFFIRM
> THEIR "RIGHTNESS." THE
> WHOLE WORLD WILL
> TELL THEM WHAT'S
> WRONG WITH THEM—
> LOUD AND OFTEN.
> OUR JOB IS TO LET
> OUR CHILDREN KNOW
> WHAT'S RIGHT ABOUT
> THEM. THE ATTITUDE
> BEHIND YOUR WORDS IS
> AS IMPORTANT AS THE
> WORDS THEMSELVES.'
> **ADELE FABER**

Trust me, this is not another 'mother guilt trip'. I certainly do not want to add to that cup because I think it is already full and needs emptying. But if we find that our children aren't listening to our instructions and if their response to us is 'you don't care about me' then we need a change of method. And if we want a lasting and a good change then we will need heaven's help.

[*Pray*]

Heavenly father, thank you that you love us and speak in a way that directs, builds and affirms, rather than tears down. Forgive me for when I choose the language of criticism to speak my anxiety, worries and frustration. Help me to learn how to communicate in a way that encourages others, and is constructive and helpful to their growth, decision-making and life.

Teach me to be an example of love and encouragement that helps my children to see themselves as valuable, rather than use words that lower self-esteem and confidence. Help my children to know and understand that their worth comes from you. Heal them from every hurt caused by criticism and build them up anew.

Make us alert to criticism and let us exchange it with love and truth. For you say, Lord: 'don't exasperate your children by coming down hard on them. Take them by the hand and lead them in the way of the Master' (Eph. 6:4, *The Message*). So please help me to 'Train [my children] in the way that [they] should go' so that when they are old, they 'will not turn from it' (Prov. 22:6, NET). Amen.

[Ponder today]

In Ephesians 6:4, Paul instructs the fathers to not provoke their children to anger. That word 'provoke' (*parorgizete* in Greek) conveys the idea of someone coming alongside and irritating, even angering the other. It usually results in one conclusion: a fight or conflict, and that solves absolutely nothing.

But what Paul is encouraging is something new and revolutionary for that time. He is telling them to take into consideration the feelings of the child. Until then, the authority of the father was absolute in Jewish culture. Now, in a new way, the grace way, we are told that fathers and mothers together need first to control themselves before they speak to their children. For what right do we have to discipline them, if in fact, it is us who need it first? It is true that our children need training from us, which certainly involves constructive guidance and admonishment, but always spoken in love and shown through our example.

_____

_____

_____

_____

_____

6

Light

'I love horror movies,' she said as we helped our children finish their arts and crafts masterpieces at the toddler group we both attended. This group met every Wednesday morning and gathered women from every faith and non-faith background and each one of us had become familiar by sharing parts of our lives while our kids got a couple of hours of messy play.

I don't know about you, but I have only ever seen one movie rated 18. It was a drama and it bruised me for life. I had nightmares and a fear of something bad happening for months. I don't think I can cope with horror movies, but I have noticed an increase in our attraction for 'darkness'. And that's not only for the movies we choose to see as adults. A quick look at the games and video materials that our children are sold today, or the teen books that get published each year, or even the clothes that the fashion industry produces are enough to alarm us about the 'darkness [that] covers the earth' (Isa. 60:2–3, NET).

What makes all these things normal is the apathy towards the existence of the darkness – and the devil too. The world thinks he is a cartoon character or dismisses him entirely. Even we Christians may doubt or be blind to his reality. It's our responsibility as parents to keep the darkness of the world and the works of the evil one at bay. And that is only possible by us shining the light of the world – Jesus.

'I AM THE LIGHT OF THE WORLD.
WHOEVER FOLLOWS ME WILL
NEVER WALK IN DARKNESS, BUT
WILL HAVE THE LIGHT OF LIFE.'
JESUS CHRIST (JOHN 8:12, NIV)

[*Pray*]

Jesus, thank you that we do not need to fear the darkness for you are the light of the world and you are with us.

Forgive me for ever allowing darkness to enter our home. Whether without noticing, for darkness can be so subtle and the devil is a master of disguise (2 Cor. 11:14), or because I have turned a blind eye. Guide us and give us the strength to not let movies, books, conversations etc, which glorify darkness, welcome in our home.

Heavenly father, it says in the Bible, 'In the same way, let your light shine before others, that they may see your good deeds and glorify your Father in heaven' (Matt. 5:16, NIV). Please make me aware of my role to shine your light in our home and world. Help and direct my children to be attracted to your light and may the Holy Spirit show them a way out when darkness tempts them. Help us to keep our eyes on you and follow your ways for with you darkness has no power and trembles at your voice. Help us to cling to your Word because it 'is a lamp for [our] feet, a light on [our] path (Psa. 119:105, NIV).

_____

_____

_____

_____

_____

[Ponder today]

'Light' (*phōs* in Greek and *or* in Hebrew) has a double meaning, speaking of natural light and spiritual light. While its first meaning is to give light, shine, kindle, glow; the second is totally connected to Jesus.

When Jesus said that he is the light of the world, he meant that we, through him, would be able to see everything else. We'd see God: his nature, thoughts and attributes (John 14:9). We'd see ourselves: our redemption through the cross and position in the kingdom of heaven. We'd see the truth about the state of the world, and the hope for the world (Rom. 3:10–12; Psa. 14:1; John 3:16). We'd see the past, present and future, where we are, the healing of the human heart and where we are going (Jer. 1:5; Gal. 2:20; Jer. 29:11; 1 Pet. 1:3–4).

_____

_____

_____

_____

_____

7

Peace

Like water for the body so peace is for the soul. We are made for peace: we crave it, we thirst for it and are in a fatigued state when we don't have it.

These days, and throughout the history, humankind seem to think that life's greatest necessity is happiness, but in fact what we really long most for is to have peace. There is a restless sea inside of us stirring our minds and hearts constantly. We try every possible place, position, relationship and riches to see if it will ease or calm it down and sometimes it seems to work or at least feels that way – still we 'awake' and there it is, the waves continue to crash inside the walls of our soul.

> 'GOD CANNOT GIVE US A
> HAPPINESS AND PEACE APART
> FROM HIMSELF, BECAUSE IT IS NOT
> THERE. THERE IS NO SUCH THING.'
> **C.S. LEWIS**

In John 14:27 we read that Jesus is promising a kind of peace that is different from what the world gives. The world offers a peace that requires escaping from noise, difficulties and circumstances that bring fear and uncertainty. But the peace that Jesus offers is very different, and it's possible even when we are in the midst of trouble and difficulties. His peace comes in threefold. Through Jesus we have peace with God (he is the only way to the father), peace with others (because we are a redeemed people we can share that *shalom* with others; to show grace and peace to others is the most genuine service we as Christians can display to the world) and peace with ourselves (for Christ is our peace, see Eph. 2:14).

[*Pray*]

Heavenly father, thank you that you promise 'You will keep in perfect peace all who trust in you, all whose thoughts are fixed on you!' (Isa. 26:3). I pray that my family and I will understand that real peace is possible only through Christ.

I pray we will seek and enjoy your peace in all circumstances that life brings. I pray my children will learn to run to you when trouble and distress visit them, that would you speak peace to every storm and assure them that you are bigger than every fear, torment and trouble coming their way. May your peace be their strength (Psa. 29:11). I pray they will know, experience and enjoy your peace fully every day.

I also pray that you will keep us in peace with each other: 'let the peace that comes from Christ rule in your hearts. For as members of one body you are called to live in peace' (Col. 3:15). And finally I pray this blessing over my family: 'The LORD bless you and keep you; the LORD make his face shine on you and be gracious to you; the LORD turn his face towards you and give you peace' (Num. 6:23–26). Amen.

_____

_____

_____

_____

_____

[*Ponder today*]

The word 'peace' (*eirene* in Greek and *shalom* in Hebrew) means tranquillity, quietness and rest. It conveys this idea of holiness, completeness and steadiness in our soul, which is not affected by any outward circumstances or pressures. It does not mean the absence of trouble but speaks of calm in place of chaos.

This kind of peace is very different from the peace that the world offers, which is a peace that comes from escaping or avoiding trouble. That, of course, is a false sense of peace and sooner or later will prove so. The peace of God is real. It goes beyond our thinking and understanding and is like a rock in the middle of the storm: it stands and strengthens us at all times.

_____

_____

_____

_____

_____

8

Love

I must confess that I get love wrong. I know that I am not the source of love, God is, so all the time I drift away from the source I tend to run dry and have little or the 'wrong' kind of love to offer.

What can be the wrong kind of love you may ask? I believe it is the opposite of what Paul writes in 1 Corinthians 13: it's not enduring, gives up easy. It cares more for itself than others. It wants and demands what it doesn't have. It struts, has a swelled head, and forces itself on others. It demands it's always 'me first'. It flies off the handle. It keeps score of the wrongdoings of others. It revels when others grovel. It doesn't take pleasure in the flowering of truth, doesn't put up with anything, doesn't trust God. It is always is looking for the worse, forever looking back, and gives up at the first inconvenience.

It's easy to read this and feel condemned, but condemnation will not help us. If we want to learn how to love our children and teach them to be people who cultivate the right kind of love for themselves and others, I think the best way to start is by asking for help, repenting and yielding, and depending on God.

'TO LOVE SOMEONE
MEANS TO SEE HIM AS
GOD INTENDED HIM.'
F. DOSTOEVSKY

It also helps to surround ourselves with people who practise the right kind of love, as well as learning to remain humble. The practice of godly loving is a journey we all need to travel through, it's the process of understanding and accepting that we are loved immensely by God and because of that we are able to freely and selflessly love others.

[*Pray*]

Heavenly father, you say 'I've never quit loving you and never will. Expect love, love, and more love!' (Jer. 31:3, *The Message*). Thank you! You are love, God, and the source of love.

I confess that when it comes to loving my children and others the way you do, I have failed many times. I have let tiredness, inconvenience and my own interest and desires get in the way of loving people. Forgive me, and please show me your way to love people well – let your love overflow from me.

Help my children to know that they are loved by you. Help them to understand that even when they make mistakes or act in a way that displeases you, your love never changes. Help me to love my children the way you love us, with an unending, everlasting love.

Thank you that we can be 'convinced that neither death, nor life, nor angels, nor heavenly rulers, nor things that are present, nor things to come, nor powers, nor height, nor depth, nor anything else in creation will be able to separate us from the love of God in Christ Jesus our Lord' (Rom. 8:37–39, NET). Amen!

_____

_____

_____

_____

_____

[*Ponder today*]

The word 'love' (*agape* in Greek and *hesed/ahava* in Hebrew) means a complete undeserved kindness, affection, generosity, devotion, time and resources given to the one you love. It's not something that happens to you, but something you create when you give.

The Bible speaks of four kinds of loves in the Greek language (*eros, stergo, phileo* and *agape*). *Agape* is the highest level of love; the love of God. A love that loves so profoundly that it knows no limits. It's a sacrificial love that gives purely without expecting to be thanked; a love that is based on the decision to love no matter what. It's the love we read about in 1 Corinthians 13. This is the love God shows us so that we too can truly love others.

_____

_____

_____

_____

_____

9

Life

What do people call 'life' these days? Entertainment, good food, going wild, not working, weekends, travelling, social media non-stop, a successful career? When I left my little village to go to university in Tirana, the capital and the biggest city in Albania, people told me: 'Go and have a life.' I am sure they meant all the above and perhaps the opportunity to expand my knowledge and see things that village life could not offer.

It's the same sort of argument people use when they say they were brought up as a Christian, but during their teenage years stopped going to church to 'explore and enjoy life'. As if the Christian life is some sort of narrow-minded, fun-stealing, adventure-forbidding sort of life. But, don't people outside the church, and some inside, think that of the Christian life?

The truth is far from it. Jesus Christ said that he has come to give us life – and life to the full. He also warns that we have an enemy who comes to steal, kill and destroy our lives (John 10:10). Let's give credit where credit is due: it's God who created the pleasures that we run after. Sex, nature, drink, beauty, food, people, music, dancing, work and passion are there to enjoy in life. But when they are used outside of God's plan and purpose for each of them, when we focus more on them than on God, the devil can use them to steal, kill and destroy.

[Pray]

Father, thank you that through Christ you have given us life and you have promised us life eternal. Thank you that with you we do not have an average or wretched life, but an abundant life, a worthy life and a life to be lived to the fullest.

Forgive me for rushing through life sometimes and not stopping to enjoy and be thankful for the gift of living.

Help my family to long for and find life in you. Help them not to waste their days on the search for a life that offers much but delivers very little. Help them to know that you are the fountain of life (Psa. 36:8–9; Prov. 14:27; Jer. 2:13). Keep them on your path and satisfy them with your goodness (Isa. 58:11; Prov. 19:23; Psa. 90:14). Help them to cling to your life even when it's hard, especially during the challenging years of adolescence and peer pressure (Psa. 119:9; Eccl. 12:1).

God, 'Surely your goodness and love will follow me all the days of my life, and I will dwell in the house of the Lord for ever' (Psa. 23:6, NIV). Amen.

_____

_____

_____

_____

_____

[Ponder today]

The word 'life' (zóé in Greek and *chay* in Hebrew) means our physical and spiritual life. It expresses a life filled with vitality, vigour, fullness, activity, happiness and blessing. *Zòe* life is the life of Christ in us, the life eternal, divine, immortal and incorruptible. This is real life, the God-kind of life in us, and it's God's gift to us (for he breathed his life in us as in Gen. 2:7).

Imagine the best life you can imagine, well, Christ came to give us much more than that (Eph. 3:20). He 'came so they can have real and eternal life, more and better life than they ever dreamed of' (John 10:10, *The Message*).

> 'LIFE IS WASTED IF WE DO NOT GRASP THE GLORY OF THE CROSS, CHERISH IT FOR THE TREASURE THAT IT IS, AND CLEAVE TO IT AS THE HIGHEST PRICE OF EVERY PLEASURE AND THE DEEPEST COMFORT IN EVERY PAIN.'
> **JOHN PIPER**

10

Confession

We probably know someone, or are ourselves, very much like a deep cistern. That is, we are not very expressive with our feelings and thoughts. We keep them bottled up until the bottle can't hold any more and suddenly bursts in the most unexpected situations and all around us we splatter the bitterness of those stewed feelings and untold words.

You see, we are not meant to be cisterns that store up old waters and circulate them inside the same vessel. We are to be rivers that carry and flow the fresh living waters from the headwaters to the right destinations. Like Jesus said: 'Whoever believes in me… rivers of living water will flow from within them' (John 7:38, NIV). Notice no bursting of bitter and poisonous waters.

We are created to confess; to empty our hearts from all those feelings of guilt, blame and hurt, so that we can be filled and renewed by the living, cleansing and nourishing waters of Christ. It can be embarrassing to share our faults, awkward to speak out our mistakes, humbling to accept our weaknesses, hard to profess our heart's pain, difficult to pour out our deepest thoughts and feelings – but when we refuse or resist the invitation to confession, we forfeit the opportunity to enjoy the freedom and peace that comes from it.

> '...CONFESSION HAS TO BE PART OF YOUR NEW LIFE.'
> **LUDWIG WITTGENSTEIN**

I know this can be hard to start. But start with God. A glimpse into the Psalms encourages us that He is safe to bare our hearts to. He has the time, the resources and the answer for all our troubles. Speak, utter or write the confessions down. If we struggle to open up to God, we will definitely be more reserved and insincere with man.

[*Pray*]

Heavenly father, it says in your Word that 'Whoever conceals their sins does not prosper, but the one who confesses and renounces them finds mercy' (Prov. 28:13, NIV). Thank you that your mercy is unlimited. Please forgive me as I confess and repent of my own sins now... I believe you will make me pure and righteous (1 John 1:9).

Lord, soften my children's hearts and help them not to fear or shy from confession. Help me to demonstrate and practise confession with them without complications or obligation. Let them experience the freedom and release that comes when we decide to open up to you, to people and to ourselves.

God, as the Bible says: 'Make this your common practice: Confess your sins to each other and pray for each other so that you can live together whole and healed. The prayer of a person living right with God is something powerful to be reckoned with' (James 5:16, *The Message*), I pray we will do as a family. Amen.

_____

_____

_____

_____

_____

[*Ponder today*]

'Confession' (*homologeo* in Greek and *yada* in Hebrew) has a three-dimensional meaning. First, it means to say, to blurt, to voice out, to declare, to admit. Second, as in different verses and references in the Bible, it conveys this idea of confessing by way of celebrating and giving thanks (Rom. 15:9; Luke 10:21). Third, when written as *homologia*, it denotes confession by acknowledgment of the truth (2 Cor. 9:13; 1 Tim. 6:12).

So, we could say, to confess is to be truthful and open about your feelings and actions with God, yourself and others, and to give thanks and praises for the goodness of God as you do it.

_____

_____

_____

_____

_____

11

Thanks

It's interesting to me that one of the first words we try very hard to teach to our children is 'Thank You'. We are happy with a simple 'ta' from them when their vocabulary is limited, but we continue insisting that they learn and use it often. It's a word that doesn't seem to come naturally to them nor to us for that matter.

I read somewhere that being thankful has been proven to improve our health, to open the door to more meaningful relationships, to increase empathy and decrease anger and disappointment, to improve our self-esteem, sleep and mental health, and to help us become less self-centred and materialistic. Thankfulness seems to open our eyes to wonder and our hearts to joy.

> '**I THINK THAT IS A BETTER THING THAN THANKSGIVING: THANKS-LIVING. HOW IS THIS TO BE DONE? BY A GENERAL CHEERFULNESS OF MANNER, BY AN OBEDIENCE TO THE COMMAND OF HIM BY WHOSE MERCY WE LIVE, BY A PERPETUAL, CONSTANT DELIGHTING OF OURSELVES IN THE LORD, AND BY A SUBMISSION OF OUR DESIRES TO HIS WILL.'**
> **CHARLES SPURGEON**

We have this habit in our home that our 'before sleep' prayers revolve around us saying at least three things we are thankful for that day, or for that season or year. We practise the 'Thanks, Confess, Help' kind of prayers. I have noticed that on the nights when we rush to bed because it's late or we are too tired to pray, that we tend to wake up grumpy. Thanksgiving is vital to our lives. If we want to become people who experience joy and strength, thankfulness must become a habit we practise.

[*Pray*]

Dear Lord, thank you that your love never fails, your presence never leaves us, and your grace is always abounding.

I understand that thankfulness is a learned art not a 'born' gift, so help me to be a thankful person so that my children grow in an environment where thankfulness is an everyday practice. Let us as a family be thankful in all circumstances, the great ones, the good ones, the painful ones, the uncertain ones, the fearful ones, the difficult ones. For we know that you are with us through it all, and that's what we are thankful for: your presence, love, help and strength.

Lord, I say these words for my family and home: May 'whatever [we] do or say, [be] as a representative of the Lord Jesus, giving thanks through him to God the Father' (Col. 3:17). 'Let the Word of Christ—the Message—have the run of the house. Give it plenty of room in your lives. Instruct and direct one another using good common sense. And sing, sing your hearts out to God! Let every detail in your lives—words, actions, whatever—be done in the name of the Master, Jesus, thanking God the Father every step of the way' (Col. 3:15–17, *The Message*). Amen.

_____

_____

_____

_____

_____

[*Ponder today*]

The words 'thank you' (*eucharisteo* in Greek and *toda* in Hebrew) mean literally 'the giving of thanks for God's grace'. The first thing that many Jewish people say when they wake up in the morning is 'Thank you Lord for restoring my soul and giving me another day.'

Ungratefulness creates discontentment in our lives like no other. To be thankful is to experience the abundance of God's goodness. It is the outpouring of feeling that comes from the knowledge and experience of that goodness.

Thankfulness is a choice that ignites the feeling; not the feeling that drives the choice. Being grateful is an attitude that we work to develop daily and make vital in our lives.

_____

_____

_____

_____

_____

12

Help

It can be easier to give help than ask for help, especially for us mums. But asking for help and giving help is something we not only get to do but something we need to do. All the independent steps to becoming a responsible and mature adult while we are children are encouraged and needed, but let's not forget that in every stage of our lives, be that during our childhood, adolescence, adulthood and senior years, we need help – we need each other.

> 'NO ONE IS USELESS IN THIS WORLD WHO LIGHTENS THE BURDENS OF ANOTHER.' **CHARLES DICKENS**

In every stage of life, however strong we might be, there are burdens we can't carry alone. There may excruciating pain we must share, mental confusion and depression we must speak of to others to address, complicated questions and demands that beg us to involve others in order to find the right answers. Life happens and spins very hard, we can't face it alone.

We are created for community. It all starts with our families, our very first community. My prayer is that we will cultivate healthy and strong relationships in our homes and then in our community, where asking for help is as genuine as asking for a drink when we are thirsty.

I understand that pride and shame can be a barrier, and there is a stigma of being seen as a needy person, but my desire is that when life is hard, and our shoulders are under much pressure, whatever the nature of pressure might be, we will find the courage to say 'Help'.

[*Pray*]

Dear Lord, thank you that you are an ever-present help in times of trouble (Psa. 46:1). I come to you today asking for help in asking for help. I know that we are made to be dependent on you because you are the vine and we are the branches (John 15), without you we wither and die, but we all seem to strive for independence.

I want to become someone who my children see asking others for help when I can't do something by myself or can't do it well. I pray that they will be free and without hesitation to ask for help themselves. I pray that by abiding in you we will facilitate an environment in our home and community where asking for help is genuine and welcomed.

I pray that my family will have the courage and wisdom to ask you for help daily. Thank you for your promise: 'Ask and it will be given to you; seek and you will find; knock and it will be opened to you' (Matt. 7:7). Amen.

_____

_____

_____

_____

_____

[Ponder today]

The word 'help' (*boétheia* in Greek and *ezer* in Hebrew) means to protect, to aid, to assist, to lend strength, to relieve, to cure, to help change for the better. Another translation is to run to the aid of the one needing help. My favourite part of the word 'help' is when it's used to describe Eve (*ezer*) in Genesis. When God created the world and all its purposes, Eve was the cherry on the cake, the completion of creation.... not just a 'helpmate' that was needed for Adam and for humankind, but a lifesaver, as Robert Alter calls her (this is a phrase used also in the Bible for God when we desperately need Him to come through).

Eve is shoulder to shoulder with Adam and without her, the work doesn't get done as God planned it, life is not sustained, and the saddest part: man is alone. Without giving and receiving help, we are truly alone.

_____

_____

_____

_____

_____

13

Trust

Trust holds the key to meaningful relationships – with God, ourselves and others. We are shaped by relationships and relationships are built on trust.

We may all have experienced a breakdown of trust, perhaps even a resulting relationship breakdown, in our families, friendships, churches or work. People may have broken their promises to us or vice versa. We may have hurt people that meant the world to us. In these cases, we must build, rebuild and heal in order to make trust an important part of our lives, for trust is powerful and essential to us living as God intended.

The first step to trust is to start with God.

Trusting others and ourselves will follow. Why this way? People will disappoint us, we will disappoint us, but God is perfect and completely trustworthy. He is the source.

[*Pray*]

Dear Lord, you are our eternal rock and courage, our hope and refuge, our joy and peace. Let my heart find shelter in you.

I come today, before the throne of grace, and ask that my family and I will learn to develop trust. I pray that we will release our hearts to the safety of your love first and then, secured by that, we will have the wisdom to develop healthy trust in ourselves and others. Help us also to be trustworthy people: to you, to each other, to ourselves and to the people you put on our life path.

I pray that my children's lives will be characterised by the confidence and hope that trusting in you brings. Let them be 'People with their minds set on you' who 'you keep completely whole, Steady on their feet, because they keep at it and don't quit' I pray they will 'Depend on GOD and keep at it because… you are a sure thing' (Isa. 26:3–4, *The Message*).

Please make us alert to any fears and doubts we may be harbouring. Help us replace them with faith in you: 'When I am afraid, I put my trust in you. In God, whose word I praise – in God I trust and am not afraid. What can mere mortals do to me?' (Psa. 56:3–4, NIV). Amen.

_____

_____

_____

_____

[Ponder today]

'Trust' (*Paithō in Greek and* bittachon in Hebrew) means to have confidence, to lean on, to feel safe. It conveys this idea of absolute certainty and a sense of wellbeing and security that results from placing trusting expectation and hope in God. The certainty that comes from relying upon God is valid because it is based on God's loyalty and faithfulness, which is unshakeable.

> 'ALL I HAVE SEEN
> TEACHES ME
> TO TRUST THE
> CREATOR FOR ALL
> I HAVE NOT SEEN.'
> **RALPH WALDO
> EMERSON**

Throughout the Bible, we are called to personally and actively trust in our Lord to meet our deepest needs, little needs, big needs and any other needs. It's a process of constantly putting our trust in God.

_____

_____

_____

_____

14

Discipline

Discipline is one of those words like endurance and patience that are a little unpopular. Perhaps because they are difficult, require effort and take time. What is popular nowadays is success that happens quickly. But the truth is, that almost never happens, and on those rare occasions when it does it seems to vanish with the same speed.

> 'SOME PEOPLE REGARD DISCIPLINE AS A CHORE. FOR ME, IT IS A KIND OF ORDER THAT SETS ME FREE TO FLY.'
> **JULIE ANDREWS**

Good character, long-lasting success and a fulfilling life are the by-product of discipline. I know that it's hard for us to incorporate discipline in bringing up our children in modern-day parenting because discipline is seen as a negative principle and as a freedom-limiting tool. But discipline is a life-saver. It shows that we love, care and want to teach our children to live in the best way. I must mention here that abuse is not discipline. Abuse uses anger, humiliation, pain and force; discipline uses love, truth, guidance and patience.

'LIVE YOUR LIFE WHILE YOU HAVE IT. LIFE IS A SPLENDID GIFT... BUT TO LIVE YOUR LIFE, YOU MUST DISCIPLINE IT.'
FLORENCE NIGHTINGALE

Discipline comes to us in three different ways. First, from God, in which he reveals both his character and our own character to us. It is very often the instrument that leads us to godly sorrow and repentance (soul building). Second, from within, in which through the help of the Holy Spirit we train ourselves to become the person God calls us to be (character building). And third, from the people we love and trust through their maturity, knowledge and care (nurturing growth). Filled with the Holy Spirit, we can discipline and be disciplined, and reap the benefits of a disciplined life.

[*Pray*]

Dear Lord, you say that you discipline those you love (Prov. 3:12). Thank you for loving me, even though I fail many times. Before I pray for my children, I want to bring myself before you and ask for help and strength for the journey ahead. I want to be able to show them how discipline is a good word and not a punishing method. Help me to be disciplined in pursuing you; focused on what you have called me to do. Help me do all things with joy and thanksgiving, without complaining or resentment.

I pray that my children will rely on you to help with self-discipline and focus. I pray that they will understand the benefits and rewards of a disciplined life and press forward with that. I pray they will welcome good and constructive discipline and know how to reject and distance themselves from people whose discipline is harmful and abusive. Help me to discipline them in love and not anger, in understanding and not confusion.

Let my family and I see the love behind discipline, from each other and from you. Those 'who embrace [your] ways are most blessed' and do not waste their 'precious life' (Prov. 8:32–36, *The Message*). Thank you, Lord. Amen.

_____

_____

_____

_____

_____

[Ponder today]

'Discipline' (*paideuó* in Greek and *musar* in Hebrew) carries the idea of helping someone to develop through prudent training so they mature and realise their full potential (specifically children).

The word *paideia* (Greek) describes not only the process of education and change but also the attitude required to bring about the desired benefits. In Hebrew, the noun *musar* denotes the fatherly correction intended to impart moral discipline and character development to a child.

So, discipline is not a negative word, nor should it feel like punishment, but it's a process (albeit unpleasant at times) that helps us to stay on the right path and live a life of purpose.

_____

_____

_____

_____

_____

15

Plans

There are good plans and futile plans in life. There are plans we have for ourselves and plans others have for us. How do we know and differentiate between plans that serve our purpose and plans that take us far away from that purpose?

As parents we go to extended pains to make sure our kids see and choose a path in life that we think will serve them well. That's why we ensure they get a good education, encourage them to pursue their talents in extracurricular activities and so on. The question 'What do you want to be when you grow up?' is asked countless times of our children. As a child, I was encouraged to be a doctor or lawyer or teacher – anything that enters the 'safe and secure' jobs category. I find myself now doing the same thing to my kids, steering them in the direction of choosing 'safe' jobs for their future.

Although I am convinced that, as parents, we are responsible to pray and seek God's heart and guidance when it comes to our children finding their gifting and the path they should follow, I do not believe in pushing our wishes and ideas, which often are driven by fear, into them. This is hard because we like to take credit for our children's wellbeing and successes, but what really guarantees success and fulfilment in life is yielding to God's heart for our children.

'PURPOSES, PLANS, AND ACHIEVEMENTS OF MEN MAY ALL DISAPPEAR LIKE YON CLOUD UPON THE MOUNTAIN'S SUMMIT; BUT, LIKE THE MOUNTAIN ITSELF, THE THINGS WHICH ARE OF GOD SHALL STAND FAST FOR EVER AND EVER.'
CHARLES SPURGEON

[*Pray*]

Dear Lord, you say 'my plans are not like your plans, and my deeds are not like your deeds, for just as the sky is higher than the earth, so my deeds are superior to your deeds and my plans superior to your plans' (Isa. 55:8–9, NET). Please forgive me for intentionally or unintentionally being forceful with my kids about the plans and directions their future should take. I can be driven by fear and worry to act as a master planner – help me to listen to your heart instead.

Heavenly father, please speak to my children through dreams, visions, your Word and through your Holy Spirit, as you did for many in the Bible about the plans and thoughts you had for them. Help me, Lord, to see what you see in my children and affirm that as the best for them; give me wisdom and instruction on how to help them learn to follow your plan.

Humble our ears to listen, our hearts to trust and our minds to understand that you are the best planner and strategist for our lives. May your plans for our lives succeed, may your will be done here as it is in heaven (Matt. 6:10). Amen.

_____

_____

_____

_____

_____

[Ponder today]

The word 'plans' (*boule* in Greek and *mahashavah* in Hebrew) means a collection of thoughts, a strategy or an invention. It gives this idea of someone making plans, reckoning, accounting and thinking on purpose.

When God says through prophet Jeremiah that he has plans for our lives (Jer. 29:11) what this verse conveys is that his thoughts towards us are for a future and a hope. The creator of the universe has good plans, thoughts and desires for us. Our plans might be different from his, so let's spend time with our Lord to learn his thoughts for us.

_____

_____

_____

_____

_____

16

Heart

When we talk about the heart here, we are not talking about the powerful organ that pumps an average of 2,000 gallons of blood around our bodies each day. Rather, the place that goes way deeper than our physical hearts go, the place where the wholeness of emotions, motives and the will reside. That's the reason we hear comments like 'he has a good heart' or 'her heart means well'. What we're trying to communicate is the person is someone whose intentions and actions are genuine and good.

Our hearts can love (Luke 10:27), change (Deut. 10:16; 30:6), be hardened (Ezek. 11:19), cry (Isa. 16:11), question (Luke 5:22), sing (Eph. 5:19), be used as storage (Job 22:22) etc. Our hearts are important. And we can know what's in them by looking at what comes out in our words (see Luke 6:45).

I know that humans are capable of changing habits, appearances and different situations in life, but when it comes to our hearts, only God can change and influence them in his divine way. Ezekiel 36:26 says 'I will give you a new heart, and I will put a new spirit in you. I will take out your stony, stubborn heart and give you a tender, responsive heart'.

Because our hearts are the centre of us, we need God to help us soften, guard, direct and take good care of them.

'THERE IS
NO CHARM
EQUAL TO
TENDERNESS
OF HEART.'
JANE AUSTEN

Heavenly father, 'Search me, O God, and know my heart; test me and know my anxious thoughts' (Psa. 139:23). Forgive me for not paying as much attention to my heart as I should. Help me to realise that my heart is the essence of who I am and where your divine influence centres.

Help me and my family to guard our hearts above all else, for it determines the course of our lives (Prov. 4:23). You wouldn't ask us to guard our hearts if they were not valuable and precious. Keep that truth before our eyes.

Help us understand that our hearts overflow into thoughts, words and actions. Show us the need to have our hearts renewed and clean: 'Create in me a clean heart' 'Test my motives and my heart' 'May the… meditation of my heart be pleasing to you' (Psa. 51:10; 26:2; 19:14). Because of Jesus we can 'go right into the presence of God with sincere hearts fully trusting him' (Heb. 10:22). Thank you.

Help us, Lord, to not harden our hearts but keep them soft and wide open towards you. And if our hearts are hurting, aching and non-responsive, awaken us, heal and mend them. Amen.

_____

_____

_____

_____

_____

[Ponder today]

The word 'heart' (*kardia* in Greek and *lebab /lab* in Hebrew) occurs over one thousand times in the Bible, making it the most common anthropological term in Scripture. Sometimes it describes the heart as a physical organ, but most times it is used to describe the inner aspects of a person's life – intellectually, psychologically and spiritually. The heart is the home of the personal life, the centre not only of spiritual activity but of all the operations of human life. 'Heart' and 'soul' are often used interchangeably.

What our hearts are full of (love, wisdom, peace, mercy or darkness, vengeance, bitterness...) our lives will reveal.

_____

_____

_____

_____

_____

17

Think

I remember sitting in a trampoline play park and watching my children bounce from one corner to the other while having a conversation with a mum who happened to be a general practitioner. I love how our children 'push' us to speak to strangers who on many occasions end up becoming some of our best friends. Sadly, this was not the case with the lovely lady as my family and I left the country one week later, but I'll never forget her answer to my question 'What was the most common problem among her patients?'

Mental health, she said, and the majority of her patients didn't need medical assistance or hospitalisation, but a good friend or family member – someone to listen them and help with their thinking and processing of life happenings. She said that once we had parish pastors, community nurses, midwives and neighbourhood policemen who checked on people who were going through difficulties and struggles, but less so now.

The sad truth is that the younger generation are suffering; many rarely visit the GP or any specialists for help. Our children may be struggling with their thoughts, the pressures of life and coping with changes of time, family life and society. It's important that we keep aware of this and support each other. This is such a big issue, but I do believe that prayer is a great start to brave the mental illness giant.

'THE SECRET OF LIVING A LIFE OF EXCELLENCE IS MERELY A MATTER OF THINKING THOUGHTS OF EXCELLENCE... IT'S A MATTER OF PROGRAMMING OUR MINDS WITH THE KIND OF INFORMATION THAT WILL SET US FREE.'

CHARLES R. SWINDOLL

[Pray]

Heavenly father, you do not want us to suffer with negative, false and unhealthy thought patterns. Please make me alert to people, or indeed my children, who need to share and empty their burdens. Give me the wisdom and understanding, the insight and patience to be an ear and a shoulder to people. Help me to demonstrate to others, in word and actions, a healthy way to think.

I pray my family and I will have the strength and courage to think powerful, life-giving, wholesome and heaven-driven thoughts. Help us, Lord, to notice when our thinking is damaging so that we can replace those thoughts with godly ones. Renew our minds (Rom. 12:2) and transform our thoughts into your ways of thinking.

Let this us remember these words: 'whatever is true, whatever is honorable *and* worthy of respect, whatever is right *and* confirmed by God's word, whatever is pure *and* wholesome, whatever is lovely *and* brings peace, whatever is admirable *and* of good repute; if there is any excellence, if there is anything worthy of praise, think *continually* on these things [center your mind on them, and implant them in your heart]' (Phil. 4:8, Amplified). Amen.

_____

_____

_____

_____

_____

[Ponder today]

The word 'think' (*dokeō* in Greek and *chashab* in Hebrew) means to form an opinion, to reckon, suppose, plan, calculate, invent, make a judgment, imagine, count, direct one's mind to a thing, seek or strive, or form an opinion.

If we read Colossians 3:2, Paul encourages the believers to 'Think about the things of heaven, not the things of the earth'. He is saying we should actively, purposefully, deliberately change our focus and think about things above. We could take it further by saying 'be fixated' with the things above, the things that have eternal value, and letting the fleeting stuff take very little space in our thinking.

_____

_____

_____

_____

_____

18

Faith

I had a bump in my left index finger, which was not painful but unsightly and uncomfortable. I went to the doctor who advised that is was 'unnecessary tissue formed by trauma, which can be removed by a simple twenty-minute procedure using local anesthetic'. All sounded quick, easy and uncomplicated. But when I turned up for the procedure and saw the medical personnel dressed all in blue and covered up like it was a nuclear experiment, the table laid with knives and needles, and a bed surrounded by beeping equipment, my heart started to tremble. I knew that the procedure was simple, but the sight made me sick. I had to close my eyes and focus my thoughts on what the surgeon had assured me and not let what I saw frighten me.

What we see can cause us to doubt. Our circumstances, our weaknesses, our giants. Sight can shake our faith but thinking helps to regain it. Faith and thinking go hand in hand (contrary to the misconception that Christians do not use thinking and reasoning but accept things as they are taught or read to us).

> 'FAITH IS TRUST OR COMMITMENT TO WHAT YOU THINK IS TRUE.'
> **WILLIAM LANE CRAIG**

The Bible says that 'we live by faith, not by sight' (2 Cor. 5:7, NIV). God is leading us, we can trust in Him, and not fear the future.

[Pray]

Dear Lord, like the father of the sick child in the Gospel of Mark (9:14–27) who came before you asking to strengthen his faith and to help him overcome his unbelief, I too pray that you will help us to believe in you, to think and trust in you through doubts and uncertainties, and walk in faith daily.

Help my children to think about and seek you. I pray they will understand the necessity of having a sincere and genuine faith in you Lord, which leads to life. Help them to stay away from every trend and fashionable theory, rule-keeping snare or self-saving faith, which all put on a yoke of slavery. Lead them to trust your finished work on the cross and believe in your justification by faith alone (Gal. 5:1). For saving faith is found in you and you only.

I pray that we will be good examples of faith, encouraging and inspiring those around us to walk in faith also. Without faith it is impossible to please you (Heb. 11:6). We believe in you, Lord. You are faithful. Amen.

_____

_____

_____

_____

_____

[Ponder today]

The word 'faith' (*pistis* in Greek and *emunah* in Hebrew) is first and foremost connected with faith in God, the unseen giving meaning to all that we see and do not see. It gives this idea of a firm persuasion or conviction that God exists as a creator and ruler of all things, that he is in control and that he can be trusted.

It is not a static word but active, which causes one to learn more, study and grow in confidence and trust. Faith is forward-directed, never passive, and forever focused on its author and accomplisher (Heb. 12:2).

_____

_____

_____

_____

_____

19

Purpose

Deep down inside of us, there is a question that we all wrestle with, but often are afraid to voice: 'Why am here – what is the purpose of my life?'

'We are just a bunch of particles floating around in the air,' exclaimed a professor of science while we both were ascending the Leaning Tower of Pisa in Italy. People have their own ideas when it comes to purpose and meaning. It is indeed an expanding subject. But if we believe that we are a bunch of particles or a chemical reaction, then what we do, say and think are not important.

Apostle Paul said that, for him, 'to live is Christ' (Phil. 1:21, NIV). It seems to me that he was living with a purpose, that his life had a meaning and he was reaching towards that. I too believe that we were created for a purpose and that our lives have meaning; that we are not accidents of time and matter but were planned by the creator of the universe.

> 'WHEN YOU FIND YOUR DEFINITIONS IN GOD, YOU FIND THE VERY PURPOSE FOR WHICH YOU WERE CREATED. PUT YOUR HAND INTO GOD'S HAND, KNOW HIS ABSOLUTES, DEMONSTRATE HIS LOVE, PRESENT HIS TRUTH, AND THE MESSAGE OF REDEMPTION AND TRANSFORMATION WILL TAKE HOLD.'
> **RAVI ZACHARIAS**

The Bible says that in the beginning was the 'Word', or *logos*: the reason and purpose for life. And that reason is a person, Jesus Christ. The Bible says that we are created not just to honour some philosophical principle but to know and love a person, Jesus. For when we know, love, serve, surrender to, and enjoy a relationship with Him, we find out who we are and what we were made for. Anything or anyone else will disappoint and disappear with time. But he is eternal.

[Pray]

Heavenly father, my purpose is found in you. Help me to live each day mindful of and thankful for that truth. Thank you, Lord, for your love, mercy, grace and patience with us. Thank you that a life with you is what fulfils and complete us.

May my children understand that you are the reason for living as early in their lives as possible and may they stay away from every vain persuasion. For intelligence, beauty, fame, power and achievement are all good things but will all disappear in time and age. Instead 'We look at this Son and see God's original purpose in everything created. For everything, absolutely everything… got started in him and finds its purpose in him' (Col. 1:15–17, *The Message*).

Dear Lord, guide my children in the plans you have for their lives. I pray that, by knowing you, they will know themselves and where they belong inside your beautiful creation. I ask you to reveal their unique abilities and gifts, all that make them authentic so that they will understand and embrace your purpose for them. Amen.

_____

_____

_____

_____

_____

[Ponder today]

The word 'purpose' (*boulēma* in Greek and *maan* in Hebrew) means a deliberate design, that which is purposed. It gives this idea of wise counsel, will and desire. *Boulēma* refers to one's resolve. It goes beyond a mere desire. It denotes the actual plan, the intention, or the outworking of the plan. In Hebrew the word *maan* indicates a masterplan or blueprint, an aim or purpose for all creation, all life, and especially for humans.

_____

_____

_____

_____

_____

20

Compassion

When the end-of-school-year awards event took place at my child's school, I joined all the other parents, expectant and hoping to see our children recognised and rewarded for something. When my son was given the 'most compassionate child' prize, I'll admit I thought it was one of those given just so the child didn't feel left out (like an attendance certificate for example). But soon memories flooded of teachers pulling me aside during the year and commenting on his behaviour and relationships with different children – indeed the word 'compassionate' was used again and again.

> 'COMPASSION IS THE SOMETIMES THE FATAL CAPACITY FOR FEELING WHAT IT IS LIKE TO LIVE INSIDE SOMEBODY ELSE'S SKIN. IT'S THE KNOWLEDGE THAT THERE CAN NEVER REALLY BE ANY PEACE AND JOY FOR ME UNTIL THERE IS PEACE AND JOY FINALLY FOR YOU TOO.'
> **FREDERICK BUECHNER**

We can, as parents, be more impressed with academic achievement than behavioural achievements. Yet, when we are asked about our desires for how we want our children to 'turn out' as adults, their character is usually at the centre of it. And rightly so. I do believe that our characters will be with us in eternity, and how we develop our character matters more than how much we know.

Don't get me wrong, knowledge is not bad, I love knowledge, but knowledge without character does one thing only and that's puffing up. So, I am thankful that my son has compassion, and I am praying my family will grow more and more in compassion. There is so much meanness and evil in the world these days, let us bring compassion into fashion. Let's remember that our Lord is gracious and compassionate (Psa. 145:8–9, NIV) and if we want to become like Him, compassion is a good thing to grow and develop in our lives.

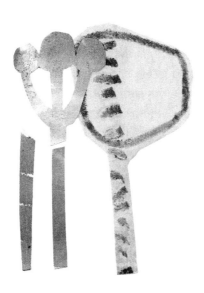

[*Pray*]

Father, you are our example of generous mercy and compassion. You are good God and do good. Help us to become like you, to become aware when others need compassion and offer it to them generously. As it says: 'Imitate God, therefore, in everything you do, because you are his dear children. Live a life filled with love, following the example of Christ. He loved us and offered himself as a sacrifice for us, a pleasing aroma to God' (Eph. 5:1–2).

Let us clothe ourselves each day with kindness and humility. Let compassion be the language we speak to each other and what pours out from us when we are with other people. 'So robe yourself with virtues of God, since you have been divinely chosen to be holy. Be merciful as you endeavor to understand others, and be compassionate, showing kindness toward all. Be gentle and humble, unoffendable in your patience with others' (Col. 3:12, TPT).

Lord, please open our eyes to see where there is a lack of compassion and lead us to serve. Help me and my children to stand up, to demonstrate your patience and sympathy, your aid and kindness wherever we go. Amen.

[Ponder today]

The word 'compassion' (*splanchnisomai* in Greek and *hamal* in Hebrew) means to show love, pity, concern; be tenderhearted, act kindly. It's not only the emotion of feeling with someone what they are feeling but the willingness to go out and help in action in order to make the situation better. It's a devotion to expressing love and mercy that is aroused by another person's undeserved suffering or pain. To me, compassion looks like courage in the service to others.

_____

_____

_____

_____

_____

21

Hope

We, humans, are hope-based creatures. I remember reading a book by Viktor Frankl called *Man's Search for Meaning.'* Frankl was one of those fortunate people to survive the Nazi concentration camps during World War II. As a trained psychiatrist, he observed why some of his fellow prisoners wasted away and died, while others remained strong and survived some of the harshest conditions of all time. He concluded that the main factor was an inner strength, which protected a hope for the future. A hope that couldn't be destroyed by circumstances, suffering or even death.

'HOPE MEANS HOPING WHEN THINGS ARE HOPELESS, OR IT IS NO VIRTUE AT ALL... AS LONG AS MATTERS ARE REALLY HOPEFUL, HOPE IS MERE FLATTERY OR PLATITUDE; IT IS ONLY WHEN EVERYTHING IS HOPELESS THAT HOPE BEGINS TO BE A STRENGTH.'

G.K. CHESTERTON

Peter, the Apostle, proclaims 'Praise be to the God and Father of our Lord Jesus Christ! In his great mercy he has given us new birth into a living hope through the resurrection of Jesus Christ from the dead' (1 Pet. 1:3, NIV). In Christ, we have a living hope; not a hope that is fleeting or based on things that time slowly consumes with decay and rust. Hope in Jesus is eternal, and it is available to everyone.

[Pray]

Heavenly father, thank you that you have not left us to ourselves so that we would face life alone. Thank you that we are hopeful people because of the work of Jesus Christ in us, for us and through us. He is our 'hope of glory' (Col. 1:27, NIV). Forgive me for forgetting that truth and sometimes falling away from hope or even into despair.

I pray that my children will cling to hope. I pray that whatever they face, whatever is on their path, they will choose to place their confidence in you and expect good things. Help me to show them how to rely on you and how to hope in you even when all other hope fails. For you are able to lift our eyes when we are despondent or disappointed.

I pray that my family will stand out as hopeful people, people who are strong because they hope in you, people who encourage others because you are their foundation. Thank you that 'this hope is not a disappointing fantasy, because we can now experience the endless love of God cascading into our hearts through the Holy Spirit who lives in us!' (Rom. 5:5, TPT).

Lord, thank you for your patience with us as we rely each day on you as our 'source of hope' (Psa. 119:114). Fill us with your joy and peace today as we trust in you (Rom. 15:13). Amen.

_____

_____

_____

_____

_____

[*Ponder today*]

The word 'hope' (*elpis/elpizo* in Greek and *qawa* in Hebrew) means having a confident expectation (connection with the future and the unseen); setting our hope in God. It also means to trust, wait for, look for or desire something or someone. It is an earnest expectation of good things to come.

Hope based on the goodness of God does not assume or expect bad things to happen in our lives but awaits the blessings and mercy of God to follow all the days of our lives (Psa. 23:6).

_____

_____

_____

_____

_____

22

Lead

I often meet people who have been mistreated by their boss, put down in front of others by their leader or hurt by their supervisor.

Perhaps more than ever, the world needs leaders who have an honest heart and humble soul. Leaders who can say essentials like 'I am sorry' and 'thank you' easily and mean it. Leaders who are considerate, just, pure and striving to make a difference without compromise.

> 'A LEADER IS ONE WHO KNOWS THE WAY, GOES THE WAY AND SHOWS THE WAY.'
> **JOHN C. MAXWELL**

God says to us that he will make us 'the head, not the tail' if we follow his will and obey his commands (Deut. 28:13, NIV). When we are focused on him, we won't allow money to become our god; we won't idolise power or fame or popularity; we remember that we are not above everybody else; we understand that we have been given a responsibility that requires more than our abilities and our talents, it requires humility and strength. As it says in Philippians 2:3, 'Do nothing out of selfish ambition or vain conceit. Rather, in humility value others above yourselves' (NIV).

I want to pray not only for my children but for all their generation, that they will have the courage to hear and obey God even better than my generation when it comes to leading with wisdom and humility. I welcome you to join me.

[Pray]

Heavenly father, thank you that you call and equip every generation to serve by leading. We can all lead others to you by relying on you and following in your steps. Forgive me Lord for the times when leading has been more about myself than others. Help me to follow you and your example when it comes to being a leader – a servant-leader.

I bring before you my children and every generation you raise up to lead and represent you in the coming days. Dear Lord, help them to be devoted to you, strengthen them and encourage them to grow in your ways. Lead them as they lead others, be with them and keep them from any temptations of power, pride and position that spoils their calling and hearts. Let the new Daniels, Josephs and Esthers rise up and shape the world with your goodness and glory.

I pray that we will see you mightily working in our lives; that you would use us to display your wonders and splendour in these days. There are people who need leaders to help them out of injustice and suffering today– send us, Lord (as you did in Exod. 3:10). Help us to not be afraid. You are with us. Amen.

_____

_____

_____

_____

_____

[Ponder today]

The word 'lead' (*ago* in Greek and *nahal* in Hebrew) means to guide, to carry, to bring and to bear. Apparently, it was a word mostly used to describe someone leading an animal by the end of a rope and walking the animal to the desired place. The animal doesn't argue with the leader; it simply trusts and follows. God, a gracious, careful and loving shepherd, leads his sheep to the best possible places (Psa. 23:1–3). People who follow God are sure to end up in places that they never dreamed of, inspiring others to follow him too.

_____

_____

_____

_____

_____

23

Will

When I was little, I was told that I was a strong-willed child. Then, it was seen as a problematic and rebellious character trait that needed fixing. Nowadays we tend to encourage our children, girls more specifically, to be 'strong-willed'. It's almost a compliment. One thing I have learnt from the culture and rhythms on which the world floats and decides what is good or bad, is that it's unreliable. What is seen as a strength now, tomorrow could be viewed as total weakness. But the Word of God never changes (Heb. 13:8) and its truth sets us free (John 8:32) to live as God intended.

I believe that we are born with a will (our unique way of thinking and reasoning; our desires and different wishes) but our will needs to mature and, as believers, we need to bend to the will of God.

> 'IF YOU ARE WILLING AND
> OBEDIENT, YOU WILL EAT THE
> GOOD THINGS OF THE LAND'
> **ISAIAH 1:19, NIV**

We have to understand that this is a lifelong pursuit. It's a continuous journey that requires a willingness from our part and power from God, who can transform us into his image (2 Cor. 3:18). Our will develops from the inside out. It is not something we force ourselves into, but it happens when we know and understand the love of God and are compelled by it (2 Cor. 5:14, NIV). God will never change our personality, for he made us unique and different from everybody else, but he desires that his will be done on earth as it is in heaven (Matt. 6:10).

I want my children to grow knowing that God's will for their lives is the best; that God's heart towards them is pure and loving and that in him they have everything, yes absolutely everything, they need to live an abundant and wholesome life.

[*Pray*]

Heavenly father, thank you that your will is not a mystery but is shown clearly through the Bible. Forgive me for any stubbornness in my heart. Please help me to understand that strength of character, authority and fulfilment comes when my will is aligned with yours.

I pray my children will be aware of their will from an early age and their potential of nurturing and developing their wills in the light of your truth and love. For when we fix our attention on you, you change us for the better, inside out (Rom. 12:1–2, *The Message*). Remind me that my children are entrusted to me from you; that I can prepare them for life in your wisdom. Help me to be joyful and thankful in all circumstances as I teach them – for that's your will (1 Thess. 5:18).

Lord, please give us a desire to walk with you daily, to humble ourselves to your truth and to know how we were created uniquely in you for a unique purpose. I pray that when we are unsure or confused about what we want in life or how to follow your will, we will seek you through prayer, your Word and godly people. Amen.

_____

_____

_____

_____

_____

[*Ponder today*]

The word 'will' (*thelma* in Greek and *ratzon* in Hebrew) nearly always is used related to God's will. It includes his gracious thoughts, wishes, desires, plans, favour, acceptance and goodwill. It conveys this idea about the good, perfect and acceptable will of God for our lives.

The will of God is fashioned and tailored specifically for each one of us. It is unique and beautiful. It is what gives our lives eternal meaning. 'The world and its desires pass away, but whoever does the will of God lives for ever' (1 John 2:17, NIV).

_____

_____

_____

_____

_____

24

Holiness

There are people in our lives who stand out. People who make us feel welcomed, accepted, that we belong, as soon as we meet them. Their goodness is noticeable. They do make mistakes, fall, run into difficulties and go through suffering, but the way they handle themselves in each season of their lives is unique. It seems that what would worry the rest of the world would disturb them very little. Their devotion and deep reverence for God drives their lives. Their knowledge of belonging to God and resting on that position sets them apart. This is called holiness.

Holiness is beautiful and powerful. Holiness is what our Lord is – it differentiates and sets him above everything else. And he desires us to be holy like him. 'For the Scriptures say, "You must be holy because I am holy"' (1 Pet. 1:16). We don't have the capacity to make ourselves holy, but God does, that's the reason why we need to petition for ourselves and our children to live holy lives through our Lord.

[*Pray*]

Heavenly father, thank you that you have 'saved us and called us to a holy life – not because of anything we have done but because of [your] own purpose and grace. This grace was given us in Christ Jesus before the beginning of time' (2 Tim. 1:9, NIV). Thank you for making us stand out as we live our lives glorifying you. May others come to know you because of this.

Lord, help me to follow you and walk with you daily so that my children will see and value the importance of a holy life. I pray that they will be attracted to and love your promises and teaching: 'with promises like these, and because of our deepest respect and worship of God, we must remove everything from our lives that contaminates body and spirit, and continue to complete the development of holiness within us' (2 Cor. 7:1, TPT).

Holiness comes from you, so I ask that through your Holy Spirit you will help us grow to become people who revere you in everything. May the words of our mouths and the meditations of our hearts, be acceptable in your sight (Psa. 19:14). Show us your holiness and give us the power to live in a way that honours you. Amen.

_____

_____

_____

_____

_____

[Ponder today]

The word 'holiness' (*hagiasmos* in Greek and *qôdesh* in Hebrew) describes something that is hallowed, sanctified, the process of making or becoming holy, set apart.

My favourite definition has to be that holiness is as a place or a person in which the Lord is present. A life of holiness, therefore, is a life lived in reverence and awe of God's continued presence in all we do, think and become. Holiness is the evidence of Christ living in us. 'Make every effort... to be holy; without holiness no one will see the Lord' (Heb. 12:14, NIV).

_____

_____

_____

_____

_____

25

Lies

The other day my son lied, and I immediately confronted and got to the bottom of it. He was reluctant at first to admit lying, but soon apologised and asked why I was so 'strict' on lies. A perfect opportunity for an important conversation.

I started to explain that the Bible tells us that lies come from Satan, not from God (John 8:44). The person who tells lies always gets caught out in the end (Prov. 19:9) and lies tarnish and distort reputations (Psa. 4:1, NLT).

I know that in today's times we hear 'white lies are ok' and 'sometimes you have to lie to protect people' but I believe that lying is a habit that births many other bad habits in life. For a person who lies not only deceives the people he or she is lying to, but they deceive themselves. And a deceived person is a dangerous person.

> 'THERE IS NOTHING
> SO STRONG OR SAFE
> IN AN EMERGENCY
> OF LIFE AS THE
> SIMPLE TRUTH.'
> **CHARLES DICKENS**

I continued my conversation with my son explaining to him that all the time we lie we move further from God because lies and truth can't cohabit together.

We all might use lies at times to get ourselves out of immediate shame or punishment, but we must not let that be the way we live. It is hard, I will admit that, but we start like we do with anything challenging – with prayer. We pray for ourselves and our children that lies will be exposed and dealt with by the truth of God.

[*Pray*]

Heavenly father, thank you that you love us even when we lie and deceive ourselves, but your love is so powerful that it doesn't leave us to remain in those lies.

Holy Spirit, guide my children and make them courageous to speak the truth even when it hurts. Help them to become people of truth and honest words. And help me, Lord, to demonstrate truthfulness. I pray I will be open to my family if I've lied, so I can show them the way of repentance and restoration that you promise.

It says in Proverbs 25:18 that 'Telling lies about others is as harmful as hitting them with an ax, wounding them with a sword, or shooting them with a sharp arrow'. God, help us to understand the weight of our words so that we would not gossip or lie about others.

We don't want anything to come between us and you, Lord. Help us to walk in truth: 'if we walk in the light, as he is in the light, we have fellowship with one another, and the blood of Jesus, his Son, purifies us from all sin' (1 John 1:7, NIV). Amen.

_____

_____

_____

_____

_____

[Ponder today]

The word 'lie' (*pseudos/pseudomai* in Greek and *kazab* in Hebrew) means to practise falsehood, to deceive, to speak untruth.

The ninth commandment is about not lying (Exod. 20:16). We might think that this commandment is only for the obvious lies but, throughout the Bible, we see that lying can be done through slander, taletelling, pretending, withholding the truth and keeping quiet, flattery etc. Satan is capable of hiding lies well and convincing us that certain behaviours are not wrong. But we can ask God to reveal our sin to us (Psa. 139:23–24), as well as asking those we trust. Only by the light of the truth can the darkness of lies disappear.

_____

_____

_____

_____

_____

26

Words

A nineteenth-century Jewish folktale* tells of a man who went about town slandering the rabbi. One day, realising that many of the things he had said were unfair, he went to the rabbi's house and begged for forgiveness. The rabbi said he would forgive him on one condition: that he go home, take a feather pillow, cut it up and scatter the feathers to the wind. After, he should return to the rabbi's house. Though puzzled, the man was happy to be let off with such a simple task. He quickly cut up the pillow, scattered the feathers and returned to the rabbi. 'Am I forgiven?' he asked.

'Just one more thing. Go now and gather up all the feathers.'

'But that's impossible.'

'Precisely. And though you truly wish to make amends, it is as impossible to repair the damage of your words as it is to recover the feathers.'

Our words are powerful. They build, heal, encourage, create, inspire... but they can also inflict the sharpest pain on others. The Bible says: 'You can tame a tiger, but you can't tame a tongue... With our tongues we bless God our Father; with the same tongues we curse the very men and women he made in his image. Curses and blessings out of the same mouth!' (James 3:7–10, *The Message*). This is the very reason why we need God to help us use our mouths to build and not tear down, to speak life and not death, to create and not destroy. The most regrettable things in life are the words we wished we said or the ones we wished we never said.

[*Pray*]

Heavenly father, thank you that your words are 'pure' (Psa. 12:6, NIV), 'alive and active' (Heb. 4:12, NIV). I come before you and ask for forgiveness for speaking words that are contrary to yours. Please 'Take control of what I say, O LORD, and guard my lips' (Psa. 141:3).

Help me to set a clear path for my children when it comes to the importance of our words. 'Let everything [we] say be good and helpful, so that [our] words will be an encouragement to those who hear them' (Eph. 4:29). Purify our mouths with your truth. 'What [we] say flows from what is in [our] heart' (Luke 6:45), so please fill our hearts with your love.

I also ask, dear Lord, that we will have the courage to ask for forgiveness when our words have wounded or caused pain. Thank you that 'there is healing in the words of the wise' (Prov. 12:18, *The Message*). May we be known as speakers of the truth in love and those who stand and speak for justice. Thank you that we are not left to ourselves; you are always with us. Amen.

_____

_____

_____

_____

_____

[*Ponder today*]

Although 'word' (*logos* in Greek and *dabar* in Hebrew) means to speak, declare, command, promise, plan, reason... it was also used to describe and signify Jesus as the beginning of all beginnings (John 1:1), and the reason for all living.

If we all knew and believed with our hearts that Jesus Christ is Lord, and that he came not only to forgive us (although that in itself would have been enough) but to give our lives purpose and meaning, then the words we speak will be different from the ones our mouths speak now.

_____

_____

_____

_____

_____

*Telushkin, J. 'Go and Gather the Feathers' *The Book of Jewish Values: A Day-by-Day Guide to Ethical Living* (New York: Bell Tower, 2000, pp 299–300)

27

Protection

Prayers of health, safety and protection for their children are probably at the top of the parent's list. I remember when my twin girls were born. They were premature, needed assistance feeding and had neonatal jaundice for longer than was predicted. And if that was not enough for any young parents to cope with, nine days after their traumatic birth, the doctors discovered that one of our girls needed eye surgery immediately. The doctor's prognosis went from good to bad to worse and then to hopeful again. We discovered in those very early days that we needed a stronger foundation to lean on than what man could offer.

'WE ARE PRESSED ON EVERY SIDE BY TROUBLES, BUT WE ARE NOT CRUSHED. WE ARE PERPLEXED, BUT NOT DRIVEN TO DESPAIR. WE ARE HUNTED DOWN, BUT NEVER ABANDONED BY GOD. WE GET KNOCKED DOWN, BUT WE ARE NOT DESTROYED. THROUGH SUFFERING, OUR BODIES CONTINUE TO SHARE IN THE DEATH OF JESUS SO THAT THE LIFE OF JESUS MAY ALSO BE SEEN IN OUR BODIES.'

2 CORINTHIANS 4:8-10

From my experience, I know that even when painful things happen, and our children go through difficulties, prayer brings us closer to God and, as result, closer to real comfort, healing and strength. We know that we are not alone. We might not understand all that's happening and why it's happening, but one thing is sure: God is with us and in him, all things are worked out for our good (Rom. 8:38).

[*Pray*]

Heavenly father, thank you that you are with my children wherever they go. Thank you that your angels are sent to protect and keep them safe (Psa. 91:11, NIV).

Dear Lord, please help my family to be wise so that when they see any danger approaching, they will take precautions (Prov. 22:3). Help them and protect their hearts, minds and bodies from anything that comes to harm and hurt them. Keep them safe on the 'path of the virtuous [which] leads away from evil [as] whoever follows that path is safe' (Prov. 16:17).

God, keep us parents awake and vigilant about praying for our children. Give us insight into our children's minds and hearts, and guide us to support and help them. Jesus said that we believers will do even greater works than he did (John 14:12). Let us not be cynical to the presence and power of Christ in us and the possibility of miracles when they are needed.

And dear Lord, when things happen, and suffering comes, let us not depart from your ways; let us trust you with our pain and restoration for nothing can separate us from you, 'our refuge and strength, always ready to help in times of trouble' (Psa. 46:1). Amen.

_____

_____

_____

_____

_____

[*Ponder today*]

'Protection' (*phulassó* in Greek and *shamar* in Hebrew) means to keep, to guard, to observe, to watch as someone from a watchtower, to stay on guard, to protect.

It conveys this idea of an uninterrupted watchfulness and attention, much like shepherds show in keeping their flocks safe or soldiers in the military who exercise unbroken vigilance when guarding territory. This is how our God protects and looks after us (Psa. 91). Even when tribulations come (John 16:33), we know that they are known by God and that if we look to him, we will face them with courage and his peace.

_____

_____

_____

_____

_____

28

Choices

There is a story in the Bible (1 Sam. 25:2–35) about a foolish man who makes a choice to refuse to help king-to-be David and his companions by sharing his food in a time of trouble. David has been very kind to Nabal, but Nabal decides to be mean and inconsiderate. And for that reason, David's anger flares up and he heads to kill him and all the males in his family. But, Nabal's wife Abigail, 'an intelligent and beautiful woman' (v3, NIV), protects her husband's life (and David's reputation) by helping the future king make a wise choice.

Abigail approaches David in humility and helps him think and reason. She tells him to not waste energy and men's lives because of the choices of a fool. As he is God's chosen and anointed king, he shouldn't do anything that may blemish or pollute his name. And with that, David cancels the vengeance and unnecessary bloodshed, all because of the wise counsel of Abigail.

> 'YOU ARE
> FREE TO MAKE
> WHATEVER
> CHOICE YOU
> WANT, BUT
> YOU ARE NOT
> FREE FROM THE
> CONSEQUENCES
> OF THE CHOICE.'
> **ANONYMOUS**

It has been said that we are the sum of the people we spend the most time with –so the people we, and our children, choose is an important decision. Do the people around us influence our decisions for good (like Abigail) or bad, and how do we wisely distance ourselves from those who'd have us make foolish choices? We can start with prayer.

[*Pray*]

Heavenly father, thank you that you have made us free to choose. Thank you that your desire is for us to choose life, to choose blessings and to live our lives to the full, that is, the best life for us (Deut. 30:19–20). Forgive us for making choices that have not honoured you and choices that have brought us pain and disappointing results. Still, Lord, you are loving and patient with us, you guide us to the right path.

Help my children to be wise with their choices in life. Wise with their words and wise with their decisions. Give them discernment to choose friends who will help them to follow you and one day spouses who will walk with you daily. And, father, if wrong choices are made, remind them of your loving kindness and your open-arms attitude towards us, for you say that if we repent of our sins you are faithful to forgive and able to lead us away from temptations (1 John 1:9; 1 Cor. 10:13).

Help my children understand that there are consequences for the choices they make, but there is grace and mercy also. The way back to you is always open and inviting. Amen.

_____

_____

_____

_____

_____

[Ponder today]

The word 'choice' (*eklegō* in Greek and *bachar* in Hebrew) means to pick out, to select, to elect, to personally choose.

Have you ever been waiting in a line-up to be chosen for a sports team or at work waiting to hear your name for promotion? Usually, the people choosing are thinking about the capabilities of the people and weighing up the options, so they can pick the best. God was different though. He chose us not because of our abilities and talents, education or beauty – he chose us because of his love.

'Even before he made the world, God loved us and chose us in Christ to be holy and without fault in his eyes. God decided in advance to adopt us into his own family by bringing us to himself through Jesus Christ. This is what he wanted to do, and it gave him great pleasure' (Eph. 1:4–5).

_____

_____

_____

_____

_____

29

Eternity

The last words of Dallas Willard's mother to his father were: 'Keep eternity before the children.' Like her, I want my children to grow up and live knowing that their lives will never end.

Eternity is a gift from God (Rom. 6:23) and it's a longing in our hearts that we are born with: 'He has made everything beautiful *and* appropriate in its time. He has also planted eternity [a sense of divine purpose] in the human heart [a mysterious longing which nothing under the sun can satisfy, except God]' (Eccl. 3:11, Amplified).

'IT'S NOT ABOUT GETTING
INTO HEAVEN WHEN
WE DIE, BUT GETTING
HEAVEN INTO US RIGHT
NOW. WHEN IT COMES TO
ETERNITY WE THINK THAT
IT'S AN AFTERLIFE EVENT,
BUT IN TRUTH, ETERNAL
LIVING IS A CHOICE FOR
US TO THAT STARTS
IMMEDIATELY WHEN CHRIST
INHABITS OUR HEARTS.
ETERNITY IS RUNNING
RIGHT NOW, IT'S A QUALITY
LIFE, A LIFE THAT LOOKS
TO CHRIST CONTINUALLY.'

DALLAS WILLARD

We live our lives today based on what we believe will happen to us in the future. If we believe that our lives will end when we take our last breath on earth than our lives will be full of regrets, fear and hopelessness because no matter what we do and achieve it will waste away. But, if we believe that our lives here are but a speck of the real long life that is waiting for us then we will be full of hope and live our lives with expectation, endurance and courage.

[*Pray*]

Heavenly father, thank you that you are the one who satisfies all our deepest needs for love, grace and life. Thank you that through Christ's death and resurrection we will continue to live forever (John 3:16). Thank you that you are making everything new and no matter what happens to us now we have this living hope that helps us to live our lives differently and purposefully.

I pray for my children will be aware of the confidence that comes from believing in you and in the redemption that Christ provided. Perhaps we don't speak a lot about eternity these days, and some see it as negative and gloomy, but help us, Lord, to speak of it in a way that portrays the truth and the joy of the future awaiting us. Help us to speak humbly, considerately and lovingly to those who are yet to have this hope themselves.

I pray that my family will keep an eternal perspective in all we do and become (2 Cor. 4:16–18). Help us to live every day with the hope of eternal life with you (2 Thess. 2:16). Help us to not fear death and not be tormented by the thought of it, for when we believe in Jesus, death is but a welcome into glory. Amen.

_____

_____

_____

_____

_____

[Ponder today]

The word 'eternal' (*aiōn* in Greek and *olam* in Hebrew) generally means endless, limitless, forever and for all the time.

What do we do with time given to us here? What do we search, think, strive for?

I love this by Randy Alcorn: 'nothing is more often misdiagnosed than our homesickness for Heaven. We think that what we want is sex, drugs, alcohol, a new job, a raise, a doctorate, a spouse, a large-screen television, a new car, a cabin in the woods, a condo in Hawaii. What we really want is the person we were made for, Jesus, and the place we were made for, Heaven. Nothing less can satisfy us.'

_____

_____

_____

_____

_____

30

Respect

As I write this, the funeral of Aretha Franklin 'Queen of Soul' streams live from many television channels. I am not known for keeping up to date with music and different genres of songs but one of her songs is unforgettable for me: 'Respect'. In the original version it was the plea of a man who wanted to give his woman all he had just to have her respect; in Aretha's version, it is a woman's declaration to have the respect she deserves.

We all want respect. I know that we use the saying 'you've got to earn it' but for me, respect is one of the basic good manners we can give to each human being.

'I SPEAK TO
EVERYONE IN
THE SAME WAY,
WHETHER HE IS THE
GARBAGE MAN OR
THE PRESIDENT OF
THE UNIVERSITY.'
ALBERT EINSTEIN

You may be able to easily observe a lack of respect within homes, schools, services, communities, governments etc. Perhaps a reason why we don't get the best from each other these days is because we demand stuff from one another, with a sense of entitlement and not courtesy.

I want my children to grow with a respectful attitude. Respect for others and themselves. I want them to show appreciation to teachers, friends, authorities and normal everyday people that cross their path. The opposite of respect is rudeness, and like many behaviours, rudeness is learned. I am aware that as a parent it is my responsibility to pray for and teach my children respect and decency.

[*Pray*]

Heavenly father, we need your help this. I pray you will help me to talk to my children with respect and authority. Let the boundary lines I set for them be clear and painted with love and respect.

I pray that my children will understand the importance of respect and honour. I pray that they will respect you, others and themselves as they grow up and become people who see respect as something everyone should receive. Even for people who are rude, hurtful and difficult, they will know how to handle any situation without letting their attitude and behaviour tarnish their respect for you. Help them, Lord, to know how and when to walk away from people who don't respect them and who they are.

I speak these words over my family today: 'Make the Master proud of you by being good citizens. Respect the authorities, whatever their level; they are God's emissaries for keeping order. It is God's will that by doing good, you might cure the ignorance of the fools who think you're a danger to society. Exercise your freedom by serving God, not by breaking the rules. Treat everyone you meet with dignity. Love your spiritual family. Revere God. Respect the government' (1 Pet. 2:13–17, *The Message*). Amen.

_____

_____

_____

_____

_____

[*Ponder today*]

The word 'respect' (*timēsate* in Greek and *kavod* in Hebrew) means to honour or value, to place a great value or high price on something. Also, it means to take notice of, to regard with special attention, to regard as worthy of special consideration and so care for, heed, consider worthy of esteem and regard with honour.

The Hebrew *kavod* is related to *kaved*, meaning 'heavy'. So you could say it means to give weight to another person's opinion… or to see if their thoughts have 'weight,' even if you don't agree with his or her thinking.

_____

_____

_____

_____

_____

31

Laughter

Apparently, there is a strong connection between laughter and good mental health. Laughter is a powerful weapon, not only serving as an antidote to stress, pain and conflict, but it brings our minds and bodies back into balance. Laughter strengthens our resilience to difficulties and helps us to build bridges and good relationships with others by playing a big role in defusing conflict.

> 'THERE IS NOTIIINC IN THE WORLD SO IRRESISTIBLY CONTAGIOUS AS LAUGHTER AND GOOD HUMOUR.'
> **CHARLES DICKENS**

I do wonder if children laugh less today. The effect of reduced play and family time, stressed parents, busy schedules etc. Also, they seem to be becoming more and more aware and worried about the way they look, talk and relate to other children. They laugh reservedly from fear of being laughed at or bullied.

Laughing with each other (not at each other) is the best way to bring laughter back into our families, work, community and world. Let's laugh more, and let our children laugh without fear or worry. Our families and homes have to be a place where laughter and joy are heard daily. We can be so serious about life that we forget to enjoy it. Let's put some clean comedy on our televisions. Let's play a tickle game and laugh until tears roll down our cheeks. Let remember the stories that make us laugh hysterically... trust me, we will instantly feel the difference laughter makes.

[*Pray*]

Heavenly father, thank you that you laugh (Psa. 2:4). Thank you that you are a God who blesses people with joy and laughter. Thank you that you made us in your image, and fashioned us distinct from all creation, which includes joy and laughter.

Like the woman in Proverbs 31, I want to declare for myself and my children that we will laugh 'without fear of the future' (v25). Not because of our own strength, abilities or self-assurance, but because you are the one who holds our future. Help my children to not be afraid to laugh; to not be afraid to have fun and enjoy their lives each day. Help them to have a sense of humour, Lord, for in this way they will be happy to laugh themselves and bring laughter to others. Let everything that tries to thwart their laughter or dampen their spirits be gone or exposed, for our hope in you is the source of our joy and happy hearts. And even when laughter seems far away from their lips, help them to lift their eyes to you and fill them up with the joy of belonging to you. You are the one who makes us smile, you are the one who lifts our heads high (Psa. 3:3). Amen.

_____

_____

_____

_____

_____

[*Ponder today*]

The word 'laughter' (*gelaō* in Greek and *sechoq* in Hebrew) means to laugh out loud, to make a joyful and demonstrative noise; it's the expression of gladness or a pleasurable surprise.

Abraham was 100 years old and Sarah was 90 when their son of promise was born. God told them to name him Isaac 'laughter' for they both laughed at the idea of being able to conceive at that age, wouldn't you? Still, the promise of God comes to pass and 'laughter' or Isaac, is one of the patriarchs who God uses to bring Jesus to us.

The message of the gospel is about even more than forgiveness and redemption. It's the only hope for the human heart to experience abundant joy and endless holy laughter, for life's most heavy burdens and sins are dealt once and forever at the cross.

_____

_____

_____

_____

_____

32

Fear

There are two kinds of fears. The 'fear' of God and the fear of everything else. I know that the 'fear of the Lord' is a misunderstood term, some see it as another thing for them to be afraid of, or some have experienced it as scaremongering used in a manipulative way to get people to do something. But that is not it.

The fear of God is positive (see Prov. 28:14, NIV; Psa. 40:3, KJV; Psa. 34:11, Amplified); it does not mean to be afraid of God. All other fears are there to warn us, scare us or torment us, but the fear of the Lord is there to comfort, assure, teach and help us.

It is also the beginning of all wisdom (Prov. 1:7, NIV). We position ourselves in a place where we see God with honour and awe, wonder and amazement, as the loving father he is. If we look in the Old Testament where we see the 'fear of the Lord' mentioned (particularly in Psalms and Proverbs), it is always in connection with seeing God, not as a distant figure, angry in the sky, shaking his sharp sceptre at his people, but in a close relationship with his people. His love is moving, his care is tender and his authority divine.

> 'THE REMARKABLE THING ABOUT GOD IS THAT WHEN YOU FEAR GOD, YOU FEAR NOTHING ELSE, WHEREAS IF YOU DO NOT FEAR GOD, YOU FEAR EVERYTHING ELSE.'
> **OSWALD CHAMBERS**

When we know that we are loved and valued immeasurably by someone in a position of authority, power and grace, it enables us to live not in fear of anything else.

[*Pray*]

Father, 'even when your path takes me through the valley of deepest darkness, fear will never conquer me, for you already have! You remain close to me and lead me through it all the way. Your authority is my strength and my peace. The comfort of your love takes away my fear. *I'll never be lonely, for you are near'* (Psa. 23:4, TPT), thank you. Help me to live in reverence of you, my loving father.

Lord, help my children to be so focused on your wonderful grace and love that all fear fades in the periphery of their sight, for your 'perfect love drives out fear' (1 John 4:18, NIV). Dear Lord, help them to be wise when they are in a situation that they need to run from to avoid unnecessary pain. Give them the ability to sense your protection and obey your guidance. I pray that all the fears that trouble them will be brought into the open, that they will be brave to admit what worries and scares them, so that I can cover them with prayers, comfort and love.

We put our trust in you, every day, for your promises are good and assuring; your presence glorious and beautiful; your Word powerful and healing. Amen.

_____

_____

_____

_____

_____

[Ponder today]

'Fear' (*phobos* in Greek and *yirah* in Hebrew) refers to the fear we feel in anticipation of some danger or pain, and it means to flee, withdraw or avoid because of dread.

In the Old Testament, the Hebrew word has the overtones of 'awe' or 'reverence'. When the Bible speaks of the fear of the Lord it means an overwhelming sense of the glory, worth and beauty of our God.

When that wonder has captivated our hearts, we can rest 'content, untouched by trouble' (Prov. 19:23, NIV) for the one who has captivated us is with us. We can face all through Christ who strengthens us (Phil. 4:13).

_____

_____

_____

_____

_____

33

Grit

Grit is defined as the combination of someone's passion and perseverance for long-term purposes. It's the stamina that makes you a person who doesn't give up easily. It's the ability to stick with things until the deserved result is achieved. You could say our talents are God's gift to us, and grit is our gift to him (and ourselves and others).

Apostle Paul encouraged the believers to 'run with perseverance the race marked out for [them]' (Heb. 12:1, NIV). He was helping them to see life as a marathon and not a sprint, which requires patience, persistence, strength and the ability to get up when we fall down.

> 'ENDURANCE IS NOT JUST THE ABILITY TO BEAR A HARD THING, BUT TO TURN IT INTO GLORY.'
> **WILLIAM BARCLAY**

To see how it's done we need to 'Keep [our] eyes on *Jesus*, who both began and finished this race we're in... he never lost sight of where he was headed—that exhilarating finish in and with God—he could put up with anything along the way: Cross, shame, whatever. And now he's *there*, in the place of honor, right alongside God. When you find yourselves flagging in your faith, go over that story again, item by item, that long litany of hostility he plowed through. *That* will shoot adrenaline into your souls!' (Heb. 12:2–3, *The Message*).

I want my children to learn how to stay with something and not get bored or restless until it is done properly. I want to pray for an awakening in our children's generation, for passion and courage to arise like never before. Join me in praying for them to have godly characters that stand the difficulties of their times so that they too are victorious in the end.

Heavenly father, thank you for Jesus, 'the champion who initiates and perfects our faith' (Heb. 12:2). Thank you that you have blessed us with talents and gifts that make us unique and different.

I pray that my children will find the passion for their lives and have the wisdom and courage to follow it no matter what. I pray that their endurance for the kingdom will be unstoppable. Help them to grow in stamina and strength with each passing day. Help them to let go of bitterness, offence and self-pity, for these slow us down and mess up with our attitude and outlook. Let them look up to Jesus, our example of faithfulness and strength.

For my family: 'Let us not become weary in doing good, for at the proper time we will reap a harvest if we do not give up' (Gal. 6:9, NIV). Help us also to encourage others on the way, to lend a hand and inspire them to finish their race. And I pray for joy, yes, let us run with joy, for you and millions of witnesses are cheering us on (Heb. 12:1, *The Message*). Amen.

_____

_____

_____

_____

_____

[*Ponder today*]

The word 'passion' (*páthos* in Greek and *saval* (root word) in Hebrew) means, in general, to carry a load, to suffer. It's the same word used to describe the passion or suffering of Jesus when he died on the cross.

The Hebrew *koachsevel*, usually translated as endurance, means the strength of someone who is ready to suffer or to carry a burden until the end of the task. *Hupomeno* in Greek means endurance, steadfastness, unwavering and unflinching. It portrays a person who is under some type of incredibly heavy load. Regardless of the weight, stress, or any opposition that comes against him, he is not going to stray because he is committed to the fulfilment of the calling.

So grit looks like a strong desire to accomplish that which matters the most while enduring difficulties and suffering as you move forwards constantly.

_____

_____

_____

_____

_____

34

Serve

From the beginning of our lives, we depend on others (parents, carers) to help us live. They 'serve' us and our needs endlessly. Then the time comes for us to learn to help and serve, to pick up our toys or clear our plates from the table or make the bed... we don't like it, we resist it, we drag our feet while we do it. It's surely better to be served than serve, we think.

Perhaps we never really grow out of this. I know that titles these days are very important. We like to cling to them and flash them before people so that they know our importance and treat us with respect. We don't want to be seen as servants – servants do 'the dirty work', they carry heavy bags, cook endless meals etc. So we prefer people to serve us. We want to be great. We aim to be first. But Jesus has another idea about how we, as believers, are to live.

'BUT AMONG YOU IT WILL BE DIFFERENT. WHOEVER WANTS TO BE A LEADER AMONG YOU MUST BE YOUR SERVANT, AND WHOEVER WANTS TO BE FIRST AMONG YOU MUST BE THE SLAVE OF EVERYONE ELSE. FOR EVEN THE SON OF MAN CAME NOT TO BE SERVED BUT TO SERVE OTHERS AND TO GIVE HIS LIFE AS A RANSOM FOR MANY.'

MARK 10:43-45

It's counter-cultural. But Jesus is our example. We may get inspired, respect and learn from great leaders in history, but Christ is our pattern for life. Without serving we will never grow and develop to be the people we were created to be.

[Pray]

Heavenly father, thank you that you sent Christ to us as a servant. His service saved our lives and made it possible for us to have a relationship with you.

Help me as a parent to nurture a spirit of servanthood in my children as well as myself. Expose every attitude of pride, superiority and laziness that creeps unnoticed into our lives. Please forgive us for the times we have treated people or chores with contempt.

Lead and teach us through the Holy Spirit the way we should walk and serve. Whatever our position might be, whatever jobs we do or calling we pursue, help us to live our lives knowing that we answer to you first and you are not harsh and prideful but loving and graceful.

Thank you that you are with us, thank you that you care for my children's attitude and behaviour and thank you that you have patience with their progress.

May my children and I hear this from you, Lord: 'Good servant! Great work! Because you've been trustworthy in this small job, I'm making you governor of [more]' (Luke 19:17, *The Message*). Amen.

_____

_____

_____

_____

_____

[*Ponder today*]

The word 'servant' (*diakonos* in Greek and *ebed* in Hebrew) means a slave, a servant, a worshipper of God; it usually portrayed someone whose primary responsibility was to serve food and wait on people. It was a position that described someone whose lifetime responsibility was to serve. And not just any service, but all done in excellence and with an excellent attitude.

It is often used in the Bible to describe a bond-servant or a slave who has been set free by the owner but chooses to remain with his owner and serve him out of love and devotion.

Let us remember that Christ has set us free (Gal. 5:1) but to live a life of freedom we need to abide with him and follow his example in how we treat people and live our lives.

_____

_____

_____

_____

_____

35

Idols

When I was a teenager, I didn't have my own room, so when the time came to find a place to hang my Leonardo DiCaprio posters in the house they ended up in my parent's room. Bless my parents, they didn't make much noise to resist my headstrong determination, but to gaze at Leo I needed to visit their room more often than they were comfortable with. He was one of my idols when I was growing up.

Things have changed a lot since then, but idols do still fight to have my attention and consume my life every day. That's why God tells us not to make idols (Exod. 20:4; 1 John 5:21). It's not that he doesn't want us to desire these things, but they are not created to be worshipped. Their inclination will be to demand all of us (trust, loyalty, resources, time, delight, attention etc) and give us nothing in return but pain and disappointment.

Yes, even good things like our spouse, kids and friends are not meant to be idolised. For if they take the place that belongs to God, the place where our deepest adoration and ultimate trust rests, they will suffer and bring deep disappointment to our life.

'WHATEVER YOUR HEART CLINGS TO AND CONFIDES IN, THAT IS REALLY YOUR GOD, YOUR FUNCTIONAL SAVIOUR.'
MARTIN LUTHER

If today we are feeling disappointed, angry or joyless, let's examine ourselves to see if we have put our deepest hope and trust in someone/something other than God. Even if success characterises our lives but we are fearful, worried and without peace, it's likely we have replaced God with something or someone that can't do his job. We were made to worship God, and God alone.

[Pray]

Father, thank you that you love us so much that you direct our eyes, hearts and lives to you. Only you can carry the weight of worship, for we become who we worship.

It says that 'Those who cling to worthless idols turn away from God's love for them' (Jonah 2:8, NIV) and so I pray that you will expose any idols that reside in mine and my children's hearts and help us to repent and turn to you. For only when you are in the right place in our lives are we are able to love, respect and treat people and things with the right attitude.

Help my children to grow with their hearts devoted and dedicated to you. Help them to learn and understand from an early age that idols carry empty promises; that they can't deliver what my children most need and desire. Captivate their hearts, I pray.

Lead us every day with your wisdom and truth, love and grace. I pray we will love you 'with all [our] passion and prayer and intelligence' and 'Love others as well as [we] love [ourselves]' (Matt. 22:37–40, *The Message*). Amen.

_____

_____

_____

_____

_____

[*Ponder today*]

The word 'idol' (*eidólon* in Greek and *aven* in Hebrew) means a manmade false god, an image of a pagan deity as an object of worship, a carved image, a phantom; in Hebrew specifically, it denotes this idea of nothingness, vanity and 'thing of nought'.

So, the act of idolatry transpires when we as individuals give and waste our lives by focusing our complete and undivided attention, devotion, passion, love or commitment to a person, project or object other than God. It's that which consumes and controls us and steals our joy. Idols want us to sacrifice always, but God – through giving his only son – gave the ultimate sacrifice to us so that we can find ultimate purpose and glory in him.

_____

_____

_____

_____

_____

36

Sleep

'You have to win the "sleep battle" with your kids' was one of the first things I heard when I became a mum. Well, that is easy said than done. When we first brought our son home from the hospital, he slept the whole night through. Since then, we can count the nights he has slept through with one hand. We tried all the sleep methods out there. We have found that prayer was and is our stronger weapon.

We are that kind of parents that 'spiritually clean' our homes regularly. I don't mean a sort of weird superstitious ritual but, like with any spring clean, we check every room in our home and if there is anything that doesn't honour God in there, we throw it out. We check the books our kids read, games they have, things like posters, toys they play with… and through prayer we decide if they are helping our children or inviting darkness into their minds and hearts. There have been many times that nightmares or strange pain has disappeared as soon as we have removed a 'strange' item and prayed with our child.

> 'YOU WILL SLEEP LIKE A BABY, SAFE AND SOUND— YOUR REST WILL BE SWEET AND SECURE.'
> **PROVERBS 3:24, TPT**

Sleep is very important for our children not only because sleep promotes growth, fights diseases, rejuvenates cells, promotes learning and keeps our children safe, but a lack of sleep disturbs peace in our homes. So let's pray.

[*Pray*]

You, Lord, are the creator of night and day. You put the moon and the stars in the sky so that the night would be different from the day – an indication that we need to rest and sleep. I pray that as night approaches you will prepare our minds and bodies for sleep. I pray that we will go to bed feeling peaceful and secure because you are with us and keep us safe (Psa. 4:8). Thank you, Lord, that you never sleep nor slumber (Psa. 121:4) so that we, your children, are looked after all the time.

I pray also, that if there is anything offensive in our homes and specifically our bedrooms, you will expose and through prayer and repentance we will have the discernment to keep our homes free from anything that influences and disturbs our sleep.

Dear Lord, protect my children's sleep. Watch over their dreaming and imagination so that their sleep is peaceful and heavenly sound. Let their rooms and minds be filled with your presence and your love. Let your Holy Spirit speak life and light as they rest, and may your holiness be seen in the way they live their lives. Amen.

_____

_____

_____

_____

_____

[Ponder today]

The word 'sleep' (*kaimaó* in Greek and *yashen* in Hebrew) is mostly used to describe natural sleep; to lie down or to slumber.

Sleep, however, is used in the Bible as a symbol to describe laziness (Prov. 6:4–11) spiritual apathy and passivity (Rom. 13:11) or death (John 11:13; Matt. 9:24).

We can ask the Lord to wake us up from any laziness and spiritual apathy and give us rest for our bodies and minds: 'Are you tired? Worn out? Burned out on religion? Come to me. Get away with me and you'll recover your life. I'll show you how to take a real rest. Walk with me and work with me—watch how I do it. Learn the unforced rhythms of grace. I won't lay anything heavy or ill-fitting on you. Keep company with me and you'll learn to live freely and lightly' (Matt. 11:28–30, *The Message*).

_____

_____

_____

_____

_____

37

Friends

He was fine as we walked to the school, but as soon as he saw the playground his voice trembled. It was his second day in the new school. Different school, different teacher, different kids and above all different language. He tried his best to stop tears rushing from his eyes, but he couldn't.

I prayed with my son his favourite verse 'God has not given us a spirit of fear...' (2 Tim. 1:7) and then we said goodbye.

'Dear Lord, help him make a friend today, please. Help him be brave and not hide in the playground. Help him Lord, help.' I prayed this with every step I took leaving the building. Fat tears in my eyes. I knew that the prayer for good friends would be an important one for this season of our lives.

Friends make a difference, friends make our lives better and good friends help to make us better people. We become like those with whom we spend most of our time. And so friends are not only important during the school years but throughout our lives.

> 'THERE IS NOTHING
> ON THIS EARTH
> MORE TO BE
> PRIZED THAN
> TRUE FRIENDSHIP.'
> **THOMAS AQUINAS**

Let's pray that our children will make authentic friendships with good children – that they will look for quality and not just quantity. Friends with whom they are free to be themselves.

[*Pray*]

Heavenly father, you are forever with us, and you call us friends (John 15:12–15), thank you.

I come to you and ask you to help my children speak to and be kind to other kids at school or in their lives. I pray that you will surround them with godly friends and people who value and respect them. I pray that they will be people who offer friendship to children who feel excluded and not belonging. Guide and keep them safe from any people who mean to harm and hurt them. Give them the courage to see and speak up when a friend is behaving in a way that belittles them or others. Let your presence be real to them so that our children know they are never alone.

Help me as a parent to show them by example what real and lasting friendship looks like. Dear Lord, 'The righteous choose their friends carefully' (Prov. 12:26, NIV); please lead us to lifelong friendships. Help us to become the friends we like others to be for us. Grow us in the knowledge of Jesus, for he is the best friend the world knows. Amen.

_____

_____

_____

_____

_____

[*Ponder today*]

The word 'friend' (*phílos* in Greek and *merea* in Hebrew) conveys the idea of a close companion, someone dearly loved (prized) in a personal, intimate way; a trusted confidant held dear in a close bond of personal affection.

Phílos expresses experience-based love, a relationship where you love as well as being loved, and where you belong as you are. It describes affection, attachment, devotion, endearment or familiarity. It's most often used to denote a relationship that is dear, precious and valuable.

_____

_____

_____

_____

_____

38

Struggles

Jesus promised that in this world we will have struggles, but that troubles will not overcome us because we are made overcomers in him (John 16:33, NIV).

I have come to understand that not every struggle we face in life is there to wipe us away; some winds blow to help us grow deeper roots. Not every trial is there to hurt us; some make us stronger.

As parents, it's hard to see our kids struggle. In the last three years, my children have changed country and three schools. They had to leave their friends and make new ones, they had to let go of what they knew as familiar and learn to embrace the unknown. It was painful for me and my husband to see them sad and struggling to adapt to their new lives. I wanted to click my fingers and make all the pain disappear. But I couldn't. There is a time to help, but there is also a time to let our children learn and grow.

'STRENGTH AND GROWTH COME ONLY THROUGH CONTINUOUS EFFORT AND STRUGGLE.'
NAPOLEON HILL

I've noticed how some children have little tolerance for disappointment and even a strong sense of entitlement. If it's hard, then it's not worth them trying. But to not even try – whatever new challenge or experience – is to be powerless. Powerlessness is dangerousness. It's that feeling of inability to make a change you really want, and it leaves you defeated and hopeless. That's why we need resilience and there is no resilience without struggle.

I can say my kids have surprised me and themselves with the way they have faced every stage of change. They are stronger children because of it.

[*Pray*]

Father, thank you for promising to be with us through difficulty and trials. Thank you that you love us and have a plan for our lives.

I pray my children will look to you for strength and hope (Psa. 46:1–3). May they cling to you when hardship comes their way, may they find strength they never knew they had, may they grow courageous as they see you turning their troubles into triumph over and over again. Lord, I pray they will know that you have given them every spiritual blessing (Eph. 1:3) to enjoy life. I ask that the feelings of hopelessness, powerlessness and defeat will not be their portion, but love, joy, peace, forbearance, kindness, goodness, faithfulness, gentleness and self-control will be their fruit in life (Gal. 5:22–23, NIV).

Also, dear Lord, I pray that I will look to you continually as I pass through life's struggles and let my kids grow seeing me being real about what I face. Let me be a good example for them, showing that joy and peace are possible no matter our circumstances. I pray we will 'Consider it a sheer gift… when tests and challenges come at [us] from all sides' for you work these things to help us 'become mature and well-developed, not deficient in any way' (James 1:2–4, *The Message*). Thank you. Amen.

_____

_____

_____

_____

_____

[*Ponder today*]

The word 'struggle' (*agónizomai* in Greek and *shedar* in Hebrew) means to strive, to fight, a struggle for victory; it's also used for gymnastic exercise, wrestling exertion or effort.

It is where we get the word 'agony', which describes anguish, pain, distress and conflict. In ancient times this word was frequently used to portray wrestlers in a wrestling match, each of them struggling with all their might to overcome the opponent. That's what struggles are, an invitation to wrestle, not physically, but mentally, emotionally and spiritually. Wearing the full armour of God is how we face them (Eph. 6:13–17).

_____

_____

_____

_____

_____

39

Prayer

'Never stop praying' (1 Thess. 5:17). I am writing this because I know the benefits of prayer, but I fail to 'pray without ceasing'. I want to remind myself and I want my children to know and experience that thousands of God's promises, which are ours to hold onto and enjoy, are accessed through prayer.

'THERE ARE PARTS OF OUR CALLING, WORKS OF THE HOLY SPIRIT, AND DEFEATS OF THE DARKNESS THAT WILL COME NO OTHER WAY THAN THROUGH FURIOUS, FERVENT, FAITH-FILLED, UNCEASING PRAYER.'
BETH MOORE

Prayer is the best help for making the right decisions. Prayer fills our hearts full of hope and dispels worry and fear. Prayer makes us strong because it reminds us who is in charge. Prayer channels the peace of God. Prayer is the best way to combat negative thoughts and depression. Prayer ushers us to the best wisdom and guidance we need – that of God.

Prayer heals our bodies and restores our hearts. Prayer is the bridge that connects us with other believers wherever they might be. Prayer gives us an opportunity to get rid of sin, shame and guilt through repentance and forgiveness. Prayer keeps us thankful and humble. Prayer is the quickest way to the presence of God.

I want my children to journey that way continuously. Let's be encouraged to pray more – that we will be the best examples to our kids, testifying the miracles that come through prayer.

[*Pray*]

Heavenly father, thank you for listening to our prayers. Thank you that through simple prayer we can gain access to you, the mighty God. Thank you that Jesus showed us a life of prayer and taught us how to pray (Mark 1:35; Matt. 6:9–13; Luke 6:12). And thank you that he is interceding for us to you (Rom. 8:34). We are not left alone to face life's challenges and difficulties; you are with us and our prayers make your presence unmistakably near to us.

I pray that my children will know the importance of prayer and will grow loving to pray. Help them to not be afraid but to come before your throne with courage and expectation (Heb. 4:16). Help them to not be ashamed of you or of prayer (Rom. 1:16). I pray they will bold to pray for their friends who have needs only you can meet.

Lord, I pray we will 'not be anxious about anything, but in every situation, by prayer and petition, with thanksgiving, [will] present [our] requests to God. And the peace of God, which transcends all understanding, will guard [our] hearts and [our] minds in Christ Jesus' (Phil. 4:6–7, NIV).

Help us pray as we breathe – continuously – for you, Lord, are our life. We desire you more than anything else. Amen.

_____

_____

_____

_____

_____

[*Ponder today*]

The word 'prayer' (*proseuche* in Greek and *tfilia* in Hebrew) means to ask, a heart-felt-request, bonding between the creature and the creator, an exchange or a surrender that pictures a person who comes into the intimate presence of God to consecrate himself as a first matter of priority. It is the act of drawing near to God with passion and petition.

Another translation is to interact with God by exchanging our wishes for his, as he imparts faith. I love that. Even when we go before God with selfish requests, or when we ask for things that are not in his will, through prayer, our minds and wills are turned to his and in the end, we get what's best.

_____

_____

_____

_____

_____

40

Salvation

I kept this word for the end of our devotion because, to me, it's the most important prayer we can pray for our children. Everything we wish, desire and want for them has its root in this.

> 'THROUGH SALVATION OUR PAST HAS BEEN FORGIVEN, OUR PRESENT IS GIVEN MEANING, AND OUR FUTURE IS SECURED.'
> **RICK WARREN**

It doesn't take a lot of looking at our human nature and our world today to arrive at the conclusion that we need to be saved and our world renewed. Like the Israelites in Egypt, we are all in bondage and slaves to sin. We all need a 'Moses' to get us out of the mess we got ourselves in. But how?

In many religions, adherents are forever trying to build a bridge to reach the other side. But it's a process that leaves you feeling 'I'm never getting there no matter what I do'. For others, their 'salvation' might be their marriage, children, career, friends, beauty, health etc. These are all good things to have, but none of them can ultimately save us. And then there are people who are interested in Christianity or go to church regularly who say, 'I am trying to be a Christian'.

True salvation in Jesus is not a process, it's a done deal. We can have it now! And it is a free gift from God given by grace and through faith, not works, so that we can't boast about it (Eph. 2:8–9). The death and the resurrection of Jesus Christ is our redemption, there is no other requirement. We receive it all immediately when we believe. It is a miracle. After all, it would not be salvation if it did not make us stand in wonder and awe.

[Pray]

Lord, thank you for saving me. Thank you that your grace overwhelmed and welcomed me into your family. Father, thank you that you so loved the world that you sent Jesus, so everyone who believes in him will not perish but have eternal life (John 3:16). You desire that all come to the place of repentance and salvation through faith in him (2 Pet. 3:9). This includes my children.

Help them to see your heart and love for them. I pray that the Holy Spirit will be ministering and working with them, showing them their need for salvation (John 16:7–8). Jesus, may your atonement be forever in their hearts and minds, pulling them to the gospel of grace (Rom. 3:25). Let there be no wasted time spent on false doctrines of salvation, for salvation is found in no one but Christ (Acts 4:12).

Help me to fully and rightly represent salvation by your grace in our home. Help me to demonstrate your love in such a way that they see clearly the freedom you offer and walk in that freedom (Matt. 5:16; Gal. 5:1). Amen.

_____

_____

_____

_____

_____

[Ponder today]

The word 'salvation' (*sōteria* in Greek and *yesha* in Hebrew) means deliverance; to save, help in distress, rescue and set free.

Broadly speaking, one might say that salvation is the dominant theme of the entire Bible. It is attributed above all to God. No one but him can save us (Isa. 43:11; Hosea 1:7; 1 Tim. 2:5; Acts 4:12) and through no one else but our Lord Jesus Christ (John 3:18; 14:6; 1 John 5:11–12; Rom. 6:23).

Salvation has to do with redemption, which is our permanent removal from captivity through the sacrifice of Christ. It's precious. It's our assurance that we are forever in him because we are saved from a great penalty, at a great cost, by a great saviour.

_____

_____

_____

_____

_____

Epilogue

'Mum, pray for me please.' It's what my son whispers as we approach his new school gate. Our girls go to school independently and we pray for them as they leave our front door, but we walk our son to school and in the last year he's asked specifically for a short prayer as we are about to wave goodbye.

I normally give him a hug and whisper in his ear 'For God has not given [you] a spirit of fear, but of power and of love and of a sound mind (2 Tim. 1:7, NKJV).

This simple prayer, which he knows by heart, gives him in that very moment the biggest assurance and courage he needs to face another day in his new school, in this new country, being in a class with children who speak a language he does not understand.

And that's the power of simple prayer! Prayer is the bridge that brings God closer to where we are. No matter what we face or what life throws at us, through prayer we are comforted and given courage to brave the day. For prayer is more about *who* we pray to than *how* we pray.

So, if you my dear friend have just finished this 'prayer taster book', which I trust and pray will have encouraged you to get the 'prayer bug', I can tell you now that you have experienced only the shores of the prayer life. For prayer is like God, a vast ocean. You can experience the thrill and the refreshing of its water in the shores, but if you want to go deeper, swim as deep as you can for it is endless. I was someone who was content with just the paddling prayer. Short, shallow and simple, and that's good and there is certainly a time for that. But I do believe that we will not stop at that. I hope that we will be brave to pray without ceasing. I pray that we will start the day with prayer and go to bed with prayer on our lips.

I hope that this praying 'one word prayers' foretaste would be just the beginning of our journey where we see miracles happen, supernatural as natural, the impossible possible and 'coincidences' that leave us looking towards heaven in awe.

So, let's continue our journey of power and influence through prayer, not only praying for our children, our relationships, families and friends, but let's pray for our neighbour, our churches, schools and communities and see how God transforms each life and every place beyond our wildest dreams.

Girlfriend, let's change the world together, one prayer at a time. Much love and expectations,

Lirika xx

PS Here are a few good books that I have found helpful in my prayer life:
Fervent by Priscilla Shirer
Praying God's Word by Beth Moore
Prayer: Experiencing Awe and Intimacy with God by Timothy Keller
Prayer: Does it Make Any Difference? by Philip Yancey
Prayer: Finding the Heart's True Home by Richard Foster

Thanks

If I wrote all the names of people who have helped me to write and grow in prayer, this would be the longest section of this book, but allow me to mention a few.

Brigitte, Jo, Taulant and Mirela, our little prayer team here in Monaco who have helped me to see the true importance of prayer.

My friends Faye, Scott, Liana, and Kate who got bombarded with questions and samples to read, and gave honest feedback – they have endured with me along this process.

To my editor Kate who from the very beginning made me feel comfortable through her enthusiasm and encouraging words, she is truly gifted.

To Sara Venner and Xenia Knight who make everything look beautiful and pleasing to the eye. What would we do without the artist's touch?!

To my children who are my answer to many prayers, their simplicity and sincerity fill me with wonder.

To Nathan, the love of my life who is a prayer warrior – together we have moved some mountains and seen miracles, babe, let's do that until we draw our last breath.

To God the Father, Jesus my Lord and Holy Spirit my comforter, you are my three-fold rope that I hold onto tightly and hope on tirelessly.

Printed in Great Britain
by Amazon